Dawn of Success

New Era of Success

David Duran Echavarria

ISBN: 9798814035967

ACKNOWLEDGMENT

Life truly is all about your influences and being dedicated. Without the push by my special acknowledgments, I would not have been able to write this book. So, I would like to give a special thanks to my mother for always encouraging me and helping me throughout the editing process and my beloved grandmother Adela and grandfather David for their constant push forward and help throughout my writing with their knowledge and experience. My immediate family including my father and other grandmother who moved me along with their high hopes and blessed words.

CONTENTS

Message from David Echavarria

Life is a fascinating topic to discuss because it is so unpredictable and different for every person, yet predictable under certain traits and morals that people carry. Yes, everyone comes from diverse backgrounds, adversities and opportunities in life making life like a set of rolling dice. But when it comes to success, you can easily tell who will make it and who will be left in the dust. Successful people are knowledgeable, realistic, and, most importantly, willing to work hard and sacrifice. Having a true strive for success makes a person more conditioned to the ambition of recognition, success, and the finer things life has to offer. No matter who you are, success is determined based on your ability to work hard and not just your genetics.

There is no real change without sacrifice; without the ability to sacrifice, there will be no prosperity. So, if you are hungry and trying to succeed, this book is for you. This book will open your eyes to the importance of being balanced, sacrificing, and thinking realistically. The sole purpose of this book is to open your mind to the possibility that there are many different aspects and entities to success and that living life trying to accomplish a single goal or be successful in one particular array, could be loitering the short time we have on this planet.

Life comes around once and essentially must be lived to the fullest. Let's use money as an example and say that I spent a lifetime working relentlessly to gain wealth. I went to school for years, got a good job, saved up money, purchased properties, and invested in stocks, eventually becoming a multi-millionaire at age 65. Now I am 65 years old with a plethora of health problems (from not taking care of myself and worrying more about my job than anything), Essentially although a millionaire, I would be an impoverished man because I did not live a well balanced life. No real memories, stories, bonds or legacies were created. Throughout the book, you will learn many life tips and ways to be accomplished and stay better prepared for the future of things. Life is hard, life is not fair, and life only comes around once, so remember, live it the best way you can and live a life of accomplishment.

To go forward with the book, you must understand what an Accomplished Mind is. An accomplished mind is one that is always thinking of ways to better oneself, complete one's goals, and achieve whatever it is they are striving for. An accomplished mind is willing to sacrifice and do whatever it takes to better themselves and always reach out and listen to different perspectives. Someone with an accomplished mind strives to be better than they were the day before. If you're an Accomplished mind looking for different perspectives and tips on being better, this is the book for you. If you are in the works of switching your mindset trying to become an accomplished mind, this book is for you. Having an accomplished mindset will be the building block to living a successful life.

CHAPTER 1

LIFE OF BALANCE

To have an accomplished life, you must first understand that life is an equilibrium. Spending too much time playing will lead to getting no work done, too much exercise can lead to injuries, too much of one thing can be harmful. Throughout the book you will see me elaborate on having a life of balance. A life of balance is being able to balance the fundamentals of life which are success, health, and happiness. Living a life of balance is one of the critical steps to having mental, social, and physical success. Being balanced is principal to living a quality life; you may think grinding a sole goal nonstop will ultimately succeed, but this is quite the opposite. Overworking has been proven to lower your productivity, negatively affect your health, and even sway you away from the goal you so deeply wanted to conquer.

Overworking on one thing is unhealthy and unrealistic. Jonas Jonasson said it best, "The overworked man was tired of everything, and he only kept going because he had long since forgotten that life could consist of anything else." These millionaires trying to sell their fake courses and who say to work 80 hours a week are not thinking realistically and do not have a genuine concept of life. This struggle now, enjoy life later concept is a flawed way of thinking. Find your meaning in both suffering and enjoyment. To elaborate, success can never be truly reached, and you can always "chase the pump" but never reach it. To add context, chasing the pump is a gym saying; the pump is a rush of blood to the muscles that make your muscles look bigger, veins pop out, etc. You always want to look like you do when you have a pump but can never get to that status because as your muscles grow, your pump does with it. This being said, success can never truly be defined, and as you reach one milestone, you are already thinking of how you will reach the next. Find your balance in everything you do because there is no finding it later. Realistically, the common person has had more experiences than one who lived a life of constant work and success but no enjoyment. Living a life of happiness is far greater than living a life of success. I am not saying not to work; I believe life revolves around working; I am simply stating that having a day off a week, for instance, and having some enjoyment in life is necessary to living a life of balance and a true life of success.

Something else that will not work is making excuses. For example, saying, "I just do not have enough time in the day to do this"? It is a worthless excuse I have heard countless times, and every time I have heard this, it opened my eyes to the type of person I was talking with (someone who is not willing to work hard to succeed and instead makes excuses). If you set goals for yourself and work hard on them, you can balance anything you want to because, in the end, living a life of balance requires you to be dedicated enough to make it happen. I have an acquaintance of mine who is failing school, and I ask him, "Why do you not care about school?" His response was," You only live life once, and I do not want to spend it doing hard work in school when I could be out having fun." I know another kid who is obese but doing well in school, and I ask him, "Why do you not care for your health" His response is," Because I care more about my grades than my health and do not have time to work out." I know this other kid who is also failing school, so I ask him, "Why aren't you doing well in school? Is it because you care more about making money? Or do you spend your time out partying?" His response was, "I want to look as good as I can to get the ladies." When they respond to me, I sit back and say that doing well in school, working out, and having fun are all possible and that there is no need to disregard each of the other ones. I am living proof that all three are possible because I have fun (having a good time with friends and family, going to concerts, celebrations, etc.) Additionally, I do better in school (I have a higher GPA, turn in all my schoolwork, do school clubs, etc.) On top of all that, I set aside about 1hr 30 minutes a day to go to the gym, having only two break days a week. None of these kids have a balance and what sets me aside from these people is my determination, ability to work hard, and balance. The bottom line is that it's best to be balanced instead of just focusing on one thing. An example is working on school grades and not giving up time for working out; for instance, this will lead to you being able to get an excellent job in the future but now have this job, with good money but a handful of health problems that lead to a problematic life. The point is that it is possible to do anything you want to; all it takes is balance. Balance helps you mentally, physically, spiritually, and essentially every factor of life.

As much as I want to sit back and stop doing work for school, working out, and having fun all day, I understand that doing that would grant temporary enjoyment but would backfire in the future. Let me give you an example, just forgetting about school for parties and such would mean I would not be able to get a valid job in the future. Therefore, having to work hard, making little money, working multiple jobs, really having no time nor energy for enjoyment. Or how about forgetting about my health and eating whatever I want, destroying my body. This would lead to a life full of health problems and suffering. The reality behind it is that even though it may be hard to balance all your goals, it will ultimately benefit your future. You must truly understand that balance will do nothing but pave the way to living a successful life. I want to live my life the best way I can. The question is, do you?

To indeed have a balanced and successful life, you must first understand what you want to succeed in. Start by establishing all your goals. There is a quote I live by that says, "If you aim at nothing, you will hit every time." Zig Ziglar. What this means is that having no goals will lead to having no success. I recommend writing down your goals on a word document, printing them, and framing them somewhere in your home. Writing down what you want to do not only gives you a constant reminder but also a vision of what you're looking for in the future. It is also good to have short-term goals, Interim goals, and long-term goals. For instance, short-term goals are something you may want to complete this week, while Interim goals are a goal for the year, and long-term goals may take up to 10 years. I have a long-term goal of being a professional (still debating between law work or the medical field); regardless, having your goals at hand is key to making a plan, balancing the plan with your everyday life, and eventually accomplishing the objective. Staying focused on the target is essential!

This person I knew went by the name of Black Jack, who I was talking with the other day. I asked him," Black Jack, what is going on with your life? Do you have any goals?" He responds," Just trying to be a success," I ask," How do you plan on doing so? His response was," I am going with the flow." I tried explaining to poor Black Jack that "going with the flow" will not lead to success and that life is similar to hunting for deer. The first step to hunting for a deer is identifying what places you wish to hunt and where the deer is, then you find the deer, shoot the deer before the deer runs away, and either leave upset (with no deer) or accomplished. To translate, you open yourself up to opportunities (by deciding what your goals are), you then work towards your goals and eventually accomplish everything you had planned with hard work.

Ask yourself, what do I want to do with my life? Do I want to do a business or be a professional of some type? Do I want to help people throughout my life or wallow in self-pity? Understanding your goals will lead you to get them done. A mistake many people make, though, is saying, for example," I want to be a lawyer" and calling that a goal. This is when the understanding of your goals comes in because, although that is a goal, you must understand how you will get to it by having shorter goals that lead to that one grand slam. For instance, if my goal were to be a lawyer, my medium-term goal would be to pass college with a minimum of 3.5 GPA, study for the LSAT and get accepted into Law School.

Goals are supposed to be straightforward, clearly planned out. Discussing and elaborating your goals with others can be salient in planning and accomplishing your plans. Discussing and hearing a different perspective can lead to understanding and better defining your ideas. When exposing yourself to other paradigms it helps as a stepping stone to get a stronger gauge of what you truly want to achieve and how you want to get there. Making a plan provides direction, flexibility to succeed in your dream, speed, and confidence (understanding precisely what's happening and what you will do next). Understand your goals. Make sure you know what you want, then plan how you will get to it and if you do this, any goal you have will be accomplished.

Think of understanding your goals as a strategy of what you need to do to win the game. You first review your opponents and their way of playing. Then create your plan/strategy to win the game. The role of a CEO and board of a company is to make a strategy to build success within the company. This strategy includes marketing, product/service, workers, income, etc. So, if companies use strategy to succeed in their daily operations of growing and becoming better, it's clear that we regular people could do the same thing with our own lives. First, outline our goal, then understand the steps necessary to accomplish it, finally create a strategy to get the goals accomplished.

Life is a giant strategy and in this strategy the balance of work, play, affiliation, and love play an essential part. It is not so much how much we work, play, or love but, what matters the most is the balance in this part of one's life. This balance will change throughout life and the different circumstances circulating a persons' life. When we are born, the love from one's parents, brothers and sisters, and family are essential, and it continues throughout one's life. In different life stages, we get married and have to support a family, or one has to establish oneself in a profession, work plays a more prominent part.

Let's take the typical 18 years old that is thinking of being a doctor. Work then takes the form of school, and more outstanding dedication and time are devoted to school and one's study. Countless hours, days, and nights are spent taking pre-med classes, such as chemistry, biology, anatomy, calculus, biochemistry, and all the coursework may take most of the students' time in this stage of life. Let's say a young attorney becomes an associate at a powerful law firm with the intent of becoming successful and on a path to partnership, with greater pay and responsibility. A significant degree of time will occur in this stage of one's life, trying to bring a book of business clients and putting an excessive amount of time to learn one's craft and be productive. Schedules, timelines, and meeting billable hours must be met. Working sometimes 60 hours a week to complete a billable time and shine to be elected as a partner in the firm. Obviously, the other areas must not be ignored or neglected. There is no need to turn 65 ready to retire, and there is no one who loves you; you lack a family, and your health has deteriorated because of stress at work. Balance is essential.

Affiliation deals with one's identity. Doctors, nurses, and teachers have a greater deal of affiliation since they belong to professions that require time, devotion, and learning. Many hours are devoted to being a professional. Professional associations are a part of one's profession, but affiliation also can be to a group, like if you are a devoted church member and spend much time dealing with advancing the community of your church, or volunteering in the hospital, jails, or schools to try to help others. This is important and takes a good deal of time and effort. You must be able to distinguish which affiliations of yours are useful and which aren't. If you're affiliating your time with your profession to make money, that's useful, but if you are affiliating your time with playing video games, then that clearly is a waste. As I said and will continue to say countless times throughout the book, time is finite, so make your affiliations meaningful and not just a waste of time, effort, or money.

Love changes. Your family loved you, and now you are starting a family of your own. You spend a great deal with your wife and your children but always keep love, receiving, and giving from your family. Love changes when you are a dependent child, to a functioning adult, to the head of a family. Work, affiliation, or play cannot neglect love and family obligations. Unless it's blood, handing out your love to someone you met is dangerous to do. Love can leave people doing irrational things as love is one of the most potent things, we as humans have. So many people act like they "love" you but would backstab you in a heartbeat; this happens often. Sometimes, thinking about certain aspects of life as investments is a beneficial way of thinking. Love should be valued as an investment because someone can easily abuse their love and bring you down or empower you. Everyone at some point in their lives will experience pain to someone they love; make sure that the pain and suffering that comes with loving someone is worth it for that specific person.

Play is also essential for a life of balance. There is a saying, old but accurate, that "all work and no play" is unhealthy. You don't want to retire at 65 and find out that things that you always wanted to do, spending a month cruising in the Caribbean, exploring Europe by backpack, or visiting Asia, are beyond your reach not because of money or time, but because your health no longer allows the freedom for a long time traveling. It is important to have play in your life. Set time each week for a pleasurable activity. Feel free to take time for yourself to play. Go boating, go skiing, go out to eat; spontaneity is key. Be involved in pleasure activities that you like. Don't neglect your playtime. It is easy to be so engaged in family or work activities that play is not in your week. Don't make this mistake. Don't leave play, traveling, or recreation "for later when there is more time." The only time that you have is right now. In the future, you may not be able to do some physical activities, and you will always regret having wasted precious time. At the end of life, you do not count how much you have in the bank account, but you will remember pleasure activities you did for yourself or for your family. The camping in the keys, the sailing you did, the basketball, baseball, and football game you attended; the birthdates, wedding, christening, and family events that you had and enjoyed. All of these are some examples of play that could help you with your mental health and lead to productivity in your work world as well, so, if necessary, consider play essential to be more productive in your work life. Also, recognize that you're not reminiscing on your success but your memories when you're sitting down on your deathbed.

The balance between work, play, affiliation, and love is never 25 percent each. The amount of time varies depending on your circumstances and stage in your life. College is great because you can find plenty of chances to engage in play, work, affiliation, and love. But it must be balanced. If you get D's and C's because you spend too much time playing and not doing your work, you will suffer because of lowered grades, precludes admission to law or medical school, and specific jobs that require a good grade point average. Love is important and, for many, is first found in college. Love relationships in college can endure for life but should not focus on your entire college life. Broken love relationships, being hurt, many times result in failing out of college, change of majors, or being denied acceptance to professional schools due to failing or lower grades. It is great to fall in love in college, date frequently, party avidly, but always remember why you are in college. You need to move on; it is a step in life and not the whole life. The affiliation you make in college is gratifying and fulfilling and can last a lifetime. You will always be a gator, a Seminole, or belong to the U. Participating in school activities, whether a book or social club, being a member of the band, or playing inter-collie age sports is excellent and fulfilling. But, again, it must be balanced against all of life's necessities. It has been said that the most you get out of college are your friendships and the contact that you make in college. That is why you need to pick a college that fits your lifestyle and what you want for life. Don't chew more than you can eat.

In the end, your goal of balance between work, play, love, and affiliation is to bring stability, happiness, and health to you. Don't forget this fact. Imbalance affects your health, success, and happiness. Be a guardian of your time and don't waste your time on "fools." Keep your friends close, balance your life, and be wary of unbalanced individuals, those who stir you away from studying and primitive set lifetime goals.

CHAPTER 2

HEALTH, HAPPINESS, AND PERCEPTION

Life is all about the memories and happiness you have, so always make time in life for it. Creating a schedule that balances your work, health, and happiness is key. It has been statistically proven that rich people normally have more problems than the average person. The rich have more expenses; if you have a business, this leads to more responsibility, customer satisfaction, lawsuits, sometimes even disputes with family over the estate. These are just a few examples of some additional problems that the rich have and prove that everybody has issues no matter how well off you are. Having the accomplished mindset requires that you have balance in your life, or you will accomplish everything but live a life with no real memories or satisfaction.

There are five types of health: physical, emotional, social, spiritual, and intellectual. For the purposes of this book, we will break health into two sections: mental health (which includes emotional, spiritual, intellectual, and social) and physical health. Mental health, physical health, and positive attitudes are the main factors of wanting to live a balanced life and are essential for success in anything you do. Having good mental health leads to having love, joy, and happiness in your life (this is what life is all about). Mental health makes you perform better, show more compassion towards work, and lead towards a healthier lifestyle.

If you do not view or understand that living a life of happiness and joy is how life should be, consider it like this: having good mental health is an investment. A stressed and overworked man will be slower and less productive in the work field. According to Rhett Power," Data from the OECD shows that working more hours means less productivity. The most productive countries are Germany and France--each mandating more than 30 days of vacation." So taking a day to rest the mind, walk your dog, exercise is an important receipt to have a productive lifestyle. More so, having a healthy mental mind is necessary for business and overall success.

Did you know that there should be anywhere from a 5–10-minute rest break for every hour of work you do? Doing so has been proven to improve one's concentration and give what is known as mental rest. There are many other ways to improve mental health, like talking with someone about your feelings, eating well, keeping active, taking days off, being social, or just doing something you enjoy doing. Signs that your mental health is poor include tiredness, excessive worries, depression, withdrawal from friends and family, physical symptoms, low appetite, etc. If you are currently feeling any of this, you must understand that your mental health is suffering and take action for your own good. Take the time to improve your mental health.

Moving forward, physical health is how we are with our body's normal functions. The definition of health is the state of being free from illness or injury. Living a life of wealth and success but constantly having aches and pains because in striving for success, you sacrificed yourself, making this a sacrifice in vain. Having poor physical health increases the risk of developing diseases, having more aches & pains, and lower mental health and productivity. According to Valerie Bolden-Barret, a study was conducted that tested the effect of physical and mental health on the impact of the work-space. "The results showed that mental and/or physical health accounted for more than 84% of direct effects on productivity loss, as well as 93% of indirect influences." Staying on top of your health could shift you away from diseases, boost one's self-esteem, and can even provide more energy. Staying on top of your health can be the difference between life and death and should be dealt with much value. Doing exercise for about 15-30 minutes a day about four times a week will sustain good health. Balancing your schedule to include exercise is essential, and no excuses should be made as exercising can be done anywhere by taking a jog, doing pushups, squats, planks, sit-ups, etc.

Having a positive attitude is just as important as having good health and is defined best by Lisa Woods when she said," Positive thinkers make the best out of every situation, focusing on what they can control, letting go of what they cannot, and searching for ways to improve the situation and lessons to learn." A positive attitude brings all the health benefits that having a good mental attitude brings happiness, enhanced immune system, reduced anxiety, etc. When it comes to the success portion, positive attitudes are vital and a typical "rich habit" of successors or self-made millionaires.

Now let's discuss respect. If you do not respect yourself, how are others supposed to respect you? If there is no self-love, how are you supposed to love others? If you have no confidence in yourself, how are others supposed to be confident in you? Asking yourself if you have self-love, confidence, and respect are essential questions! Your self-esteem or a positive outlook could be lacking if you answered no to any of those questions. A positive attitude will lead to more love and affection towards yourself, boosting your confidence and leading to endless amounts of self-growth. Going into anything with the mindset that you will fail will ultimately lead to your demise. Surround yourself with positive people, focus on the present, talk good to yourself, practice gratitude, and be a positive person. You will notice significant changes in happiness, mental health, success, and self-growth in doing this.

Everything you do runs through your mind and having a negative or mentally unhealthy sense of things will manifest in your work and have a trickle effect in many areas of your life. Treat yourself like you would treat a new car and be mindful. You are the most valuable thing in the world and must be viewed as so. Putting your health at risk is not worth any success in this world. If your path to success requires you to kill yourself virtually then, your approach should be revaluated into a balanced life cycle that leads to success, proper mental health, and happiness.

Now the reality of things; all reality is inner analyzed. To have an accomplished mind, you must first understand the reality and truth behind scenarios. Reality is not always what happens realistically and can be out of our control. Reality is nothing more, but our perception of what happens, and its beauty is that everybody has a different perception. A common mistake is personalizing every mistake as our own when caused by factors that we can't control. There will always be events in the world affecting you, like a pandemic, a war, a recession, or just a general illness or an accident that you encounter. What makes a difference is your perception of the event? All events happen, you process the event in your mind, with your evaluations and expectations, and you come to a conclusion. For example, you were working in a restaurant as a waiter, and you were laid off because of the pandemic. Something unexpected happened, and now you have to make of it. You can internally decide that you had no power over this event and just cry and go homeless, but you have the ability to process it. Obviously, you will be shocked at first. You can decide to use your resources to plan for a new job either in same area or other areas, like areas that you always wanted, for example, let's say you wanted to always work at the casino as a Black Jack dealer, a job that you admire for the excitement, better pay, and better tips. Now you are in a better scenario because you processed reality and moved along instead of slouching down and falling apart. Sometimes these unexpected changes are life-changers. Also, you can use the downtime to spend time doing something that you could not do because of the job. Now you can concentrate on family, yourself, working out, losing weight, getting fit, or educating yourself for a new job like being a nurse or teacher, something that you always wished you could do. Perhaps, you can move to the dream city you always wanted to live in or just get out of the rut you were in, either in a relationship, business, or living arrangement. In essence, an unexpected bad event can be internally processed as something else. Emotions and plans don't need to happen automatically. Your thinking and reactions need to be processed by you internally as you wish to be. The power of positive thinking is underestimated in our society.

Let me tell you a funny story from when I was in NYC. I was riding the subway in NYC during a busy hour, and then I stood up and suddenly felt a push on my back. My automatic response was, I am being mugged", or "what the hell, keep your space." You automatically feel angry and ready to defend yourself and strike back. However, I turned around and saw an elderly lady, heavily loaded with groceries, who stumbled into me because the subway made a sudden move. Now my reaction was one of succor and sympathy. By this example, one can see where automatic responses are brisk and unnecessary. Better to access your situation differently, rationally, and calmly. Life is constantly shifting in the blink of an eye and we need to change the things we can change, accept those we cannot, and understand the difference. We are more than just parts; we are more than the sum of our parts; we are unique beings with the ability and desire to move beyond the circumstances that we are in now.

Reality and the outcome of things are determined by your perception of the scenario and then your actions that go in accordance with your perception. So, to be a success and live a balanced lifestyle, you need to change your perspective. Having a positive perception will lead to having positive outcomes. They say when you go into something with the mentality that you will fail, you will fail. So, falling apart after something unpleasant happens should not be your initial reaction; instead, you should be finding ways to recover and be better than you were before the specific scenario occurred. Reality is what you make of it, so mold it in a way that will keep you happy, healthy, and prosperous.

Everyone has a different perspective on things. Let's say you are looking at a painting and focus on more of the waterfall and perceive the painting as a beautiful graphic of the wilderness; someone else may perceive it as a flow of feelings going down the waterfall and into their heart. The outlook is that you may see something one way while someone sees it in another. Understanding that there are different perspectives and ideas is a crucial part of living a life of success. If you never hear other perspectives and stay in your own train of thought, you will never grow as a person or from a business standpoint. Let's say you are thinking of approaching a work problem one way, but you evaluate it with a friend and find an even better approach, one you never thought of before. Understanding that there is not only one right way of doing things will lower how stubborn one becomes (stubbornness being a trait that holds people back). To be a success, you must be adaptable and able to grow continuously and at a more rapid pace than the sum of society.

When people hire employees for certain positions, they look for people who perceive things differently. For example, let us use Jeff Bezos; he thought of Amazon, which was an idea nobody had heard of before. When he explained his idea to investors, they did not believe in it, not understanding his perspective that the internet was the next big thing. His perseverance, hard work, and belief in his vision made Amazon come to life after many years of struggling to find investors. However, the right group of individuals looked beyond the ordinary and saw an extraordinary opportunity to create a new market; to create change.

When companies do not take the time to do self-analysis to see how they need to adapt, change, and do professionally develop, they are risking failure; complete financial ruin. In the same demeanor, we as individuals risk the same dangers as major companies if we do not keep up with our professional development and educational growth. Let's take a look at Blockbuster; they thought their DVDs were the best thing around even while Netflix and online television became more and more popular. Again, they didn't perceive the situation the correct way and went bankrupt. Something which could have possibly been avoided through professional assessments and collection of data to give the CEO's

multiple perspectives on how to take the company to the next level.

The daily life of a human being can be described as a roller

coaster; it is full of an array of emotions and many different obstacles

that one must encounter. As a young adult, this roller coaster ride

may seem overpowering at times, like the "El Toro" ride in Six Flags

Great Adventure. However, like in other areas in life, balancing one's

emotions is essential to ultimately having the most fulfilling, well-

rounded life. Unfortunately, society often puts a negative stigma on

people whose rollercoaster is more convoluted with twists and turns

because they are too emotional. Still, the bottom line is that young

people can't be shamed for how they feel. Your emotions are a part

of your imprint, how you are feeling in that moment in time, and

there is nothing wrong with that. All emotions are good; the problem

might be how we react to specific emotions. As mentioned in other

sections of this book, balance is a fundamental aspect of success.

Balancing our emotions is no expectation!

Our body is an intricate system that is constantly sending us

messages. The better we learn to listen and decode these messages

our body tells us; we will become healthier. For example, suppose a person feels gloomy, anxious, and eerie every time they are peer pressured by their friends, fraternity, or sorority to belittle or undermine a stereotypical group of people in school. In that case, they should not suppress those emotions. Those negative emotions being experienced are key cues that alert them to reflect on the situation being encountered. Often when the steps are taken to reflect on a situation that is producing negative emotions and feelings within us, we can determine that in the core of the problem we were phasing essentially, we were acting against the fundamental values that were instilled in us. One must take a few minutes after a situation where we felt that we lost our inner zing and realign ourselves before carrying on with the next task. Stress is a part of our daily lives, and everyone must find their stress relief mechanism or approach to try to live a well-balanced life.

When not under control, our emotions can have an adverse effect on our physical and mental health, social life, relationships, school, work, and hobbies, to name a few areas. Therefore, it is critical and imperative that individuals have a sound support system. As I often hear my mom says, "it takes a village to raise a child." However, that concept is not inclusive to children; everyone needs a good backbone to support them and guide them in the path of life.

CHAPTER 3

LIFETIME INVESTMENTS

The biggest investment in life is your knowledge and understanding. To truly be a success you must become an entirely different person with certain traits and understanding of things. All the most successful people in the world all carry similar traits and characteristics while the unsuccessful carry their similar traits as well. Throughout this chapter you will learn concepts past the traditional and more into some of the more complicated or simplistic concepts that are necessities to understand and become a success in life.

Work, or the ability to work for remuneration, is one of the most essential tasks we encounter in life, and while working, you must have a "Free for all" mentality. The reality behind it is that you do not need a business to succeed, and most people will have to do work for other people or corporations. Generally, not only is work such an important task, but it is the most significant investment we make for ourselves throughout our lifespan. For the most part, we spend the first 20- 25 years of our life in school studying to prepare for the workforce. Then, we acquire the job and work another 40-50 years trying to climb up the ladder and be successful. Nothing in our life requires as much effort or time as the job path we choose to follow. Even time with the family, enjoyable activities, hobbies don't take as much time or effort. People typically work 50 weeks out of the year with only two weeks for vacations, for those who are lucky to afford the time or the money to take those two weeks off. Many people feel exhausted, fatigued, frustrated, and sometimes depressed due to lack of success at work, being overworked, underappreciated, and oftentimes underpaid. People need to keep and maintain a home, paying the bills, dealing with prior loans commitment, and taking care of their families. In the past, think 1950 or 1960, one single salary was sufficient to maintain a home and a family. Today, most families require two wages, or at least someone working full time and a part-time job, to provide bare necessities, like a roof over one's head and food on the table.

In the past, employers had loyalty for employees, and

employees had loyalty to the company. In the past, there were "FORD men; IBM men." Now, employers look at their employees no better than a cost; rent, a machine, a cost to minimize. There are downsides to working like getting laid off due to technological advances, consolidation of business, when two companies consolidate, massive layoffs of employees are done. You must live for yourself and remember business is business; you need money in your pockets over everything (this is how people think and will throw you under the bus for a pretty penny).

The way to cope with this "dog eat dog" mentality is not easy; first, you must look at an industry or employer with a reputation for employee satisfaction and high pay and benefits. Unfortunately, there are not many around; only priests, teachers, first responders, firefighters and police officers, are having some consideration for working conditions, benefits, retirements, and tenure at work. This is related to a "thankless and low paying job," that include teachers and priests, or strong unions; like policemen and firemen. Most of the rest of the workers can be "hired on Monday and Fired on Wednesday." It is easy to give more incentives and benefits when you are not paying your employees as much as someone in the private sector would get. Employees have become astute and forced to "look for number one." If you are not compensated well, look for a better deal, for example, higher pay, better working conditions, and better job security. The idea of being a "FORD man" is over. Employees need to be in tune with the possibility in their industry and be able to jump ship as needed. It is usual for employees to change jobs every three to four years to increase salary or working conditions. This requires the employee to be "up to date" on the trends and expertise needed in their individual jobs. Everyone is competing with you for your job so, once you have a profession picked out, take full advantage of it by training, networking, attending job-related conventions, and generally, keeping your eyes open for a better position.

The company is not your friend or your family, regardless of what they tell you. Employees need to look for the number one spot and seek their best opportunity. It is human nature to live for oneself and try to survive by any means possible. This being said, do whatever it takes to benefit yourself. A typical scenario is that you should be heading for the door if you have been passed over or declined twice for a salary increase or promotion. Also, if another company offers you more than a 15 percent increase over your salary, you should jump ship, since likely your company may take 4 to 6 years to increase at that level. Being still and not moving ahead is a downward step, and not moving forward. Royalty to the company and company loyalty to employees is dead and buried. It is likely that in the typical 40-year work life, an employee will "jump ship" every four years, having 10 to 12 different jobs. Also, industry changes, and jobs change with them. Employees need to be technological up to date, with suitable job skills. Many people start in a position, and ten years later, they are doing something completely different from their original job. This is healthy and likely results in promotions or career changes. In essence, one needs to put the family's needs first and not have a dogmatic loyalty to a company or industry when reality does not care about you as a person. Be ready to "jump ship" for a better job, don't let your work skills stagnate, maintain current by training and upgrading, keep networking and developing contacts in your current industry or another industry that you want to explore to increase salary and work conditions. The rule of 7 indicates that you should be doubling your salary, or going up at least 70%, every seven years. Otherwise, you fall behind inflation and would not sustain your family, residence, education, and other goals. Don't stay in a job because you get a tap on your head when what you need is a tap in your pockets, with more money. You are not a priest, and there is no special place in heaven for your profession.

A good progression in any job is that once hired, the first year is getting to do your job professionally, ethically, and efficiently, and making the necessary adjustments to "get the job done" well, timely, and effectively. The second year in the job is making improvements to the job and the company, bringing profit and efficiency to the job and tasks, without any waste of resources. The third-year is getting a promotion and hopefully a minimal 30 percent increase in salary and benefits. In the first year, you should request an evaluation of your performance about every six months, with satisfactory performance requesting a 5 to 10 percent increase in pay, the second year, you can request a yearly performance review, with a 10 percent increase with satisfactory performance, and this should be done every year, for instance, an annual evaluation with 10 percent increase in salary. From then on, look for opportunities, and be alert to any possibility of rapid increases in salary and benefits with your company or another company that sees your worth and production.

Every life has ups and downs. We need to play the cards that we are dealt. Like in poker, one will not always get Poker AA or KK to play, and sometimes opportunity will not come our way. We need to develop and foster those opportunities. Success is sometimes being at the right place at the right time or having the right connections. These need to develop. One will need to foster those opportunities that come our way and nurture those friendships and relationships that enhance life, bring happiness, and care about us. Divorce and marriage are some of those areas. A well-balanced marriage will bring happiness and calm the storm and allow one to concentrate on moving ahead, planning, and taking calculated risks. A divorce is a total distraction, with financial hardships, like alimony, child support, and an overall, downward, and frustrating experience that can be avoided by making calculated preset arrangements ahead of the storm reducing the calamities should such an event arise.

Divorce results in emotional pain, financial frustration, and energy spent trying to readjust and reinitiate life. It typically results in a turmoil of strains. Relationships must be treated as investments, cut losses short on those unproductive ones, those relationships that don't add to your life, finances, or happiness. However, those who enrich your life need to be nurtured, fostered, and looked out after, like you would do with any vital investment or entity in life. Relationships are never 50/50 but you need to foster a healthy balance of reciprocity where you each provide for each other's needs.

Marriage requires careful planning as being married can lead to you prospering as a person/ being successful or can be your downfall and take half of everything you have worked for. Life is very unexpected, and even though you may think you have "The One," it is still wise to protect your assets. Marriage is a high-risk, high reward investment, but there are ways to minimize the risk. Creating a prenuptial can help protect you and your assets just in case of a divorce. In simple terms, a prenuptial agreement protects you financially from your spouse. The Prenuptial agreement determines issues like how property is divided, alimony, etc. Prenuptial agreements can also protect the income you receive during the marriage and is the safest thing to do to protect yourself during this "Investment."

Before you get married, make sure to get a deep understanding of the person you want to spend the rest of your life with. Make sure you guys are in-line with certain topics like expectations of having children and problems that come along with them (how they will be handled financially and who will care for them), financial goals, how to deal with issues together, etc. Before marriage, you and your partner have good communications, know their finances, understand your partner (deal-breakers, fears, attitude, reactions), move in with your partner (know how they are around the house), etc. The average couple is in a relationship for five years before marriage, which is the perfect time to understand your partner truly. To conclude, marriage (like any other investment) should be carefully investigated and protected as all assets have risks and can fail.

To move forward, another significant investment throughout life that many people don't even know consider an investment is your friends. Choosing friends wisely will help you grow as a person but choosing the wrong friends can be detrimental with everlasting effects. I know plenty of people, and I try to be friendly and merrymaking with everyone but, people are under the impression that we are friends and that everyone they associate with is their friend. This assumption that these people have is wrong because a friend should give you good times, but also (similar to having a partner in a relationship) respects you, are loyal to you, helps you grow, etc. I would categorize most of the people I interact with as an associate or acquaintance not a friend. So, ask yourself, do you know the people you are hanging out with enough to be able to call them a friend? Or are they just acquaintances? Most of the people around you right now (other than family) are temporary, and as soon as your paths depart, you will never hear from them again. The people who listen to you and reach out when you part ways, the ones who have your back, are your true friends. Even with my friends whom I have known for years, their friendship has never been genuinely tested, so I frankly cannot call them close friends.

A scenario that teaches most people about true friends is going to college. You have partied, studied, talked with, laughed, played sports with hundreds of people in high school, but as soon as you go off to college, you may see these people a few years later, but your relationships ultimately fade. Friends (for the most part) are temporary and provide good times and support when things are bad, but something people do not look for in friends that should be one of the essential things is growth. A friend who helps you grow is one that you should keep by your side as long as you can. The old saying goes that if you hang out with three successful people, you will be the next, but if you hang out with three bums, you will be the 4th. Look deeply into whom you hang around with and consider what they bring to the table and how they will help you grow. A friend who is constantly doing drugs or criminal activity will drag you down. The truth behind it is you never honestly know whom you could trust, friends and family alike. I heard of this story on the news that an Aunt gave her nephew a lottery ticket for his birthday. He scratched off the ticket and hit the million-dollar jackpot and was kind enough to split the earnings 50/50 with his aunt. On the other hand, the aunt was not so good-hearted and sued her nephew with the argument that she gave the ticket to him with the understanding that he could keep the winnings for all the other prizes except the jackpot. This being said, putting all your time and trust into anybody is a mistake. I have had good friends whom I thought would never betray me, and they destroyed their loyalty and /trust with me over a quick dollar. It is human nature to want more and live better, so if a "friend" is in your block for the path towards success, most people will show their disloyalty and screw over their buddy. Live for yourself because friends come and go. Make sure while your friends are around, though, you learn from them, they help you grow, respect you, and you enjoy your time with them. All relationships are about reciprocity and if you seek to have fruitful relationships you must reciprocate and nurture those friendships so they may blossom and sprout into lifelong bonds that you can count on.

As much as friends and family are important to have throughout life, never rely on anybody too much. A quick example is relying on someone emotionally for happiness which means that your joy runs through this person. If this person fails to make you happy, you will be disappointed and depressed. Another example could be relying on parents for money or necessities will make it harder for you to survive when you eventually take the first steps of living an adult life. Understand that you must learn to be independent, and this will help you live a better, more balanced life. You must balance socializing with others and doing things on your own. If you rely on others to do everything for you, your skillset is nothing without them by your side. This decreases your self-worth and your ability to live life in general.

Now we move onto our time; live with purpose. Life is finite, and time is of the essence, so do not do things without it genuinely benefiting you. Try continuously being as productive as possible, always tie your actions with your goals. All actions should be aligned towards your short term or long-term goals to ensure you are living a well-rounded life. I have my own schedule which I stick to everyday making me as productive as possible. Evaluating my schedule makes it clear that everything I do throughout the day is helping me with a particular aspect of myself and that there is no time to waste doing purposeless things such as watching Netflix or playing video games.

Let's say that you finished a long day of work; now you have to work on your other goals, one of your goals being to become slimmer so, you go on and workout instead of sitting down and watching Netflix which brings you no personal gains. Personally, I think video games, TV, scrolling through Tik-Tok, are all examples of instant gratifications which should be sacrificed and replaced with more productive activities that lead towards personal gains. You can even combine your health with happiness for instance if you enjoy basketball, you could use this option. Basketball in this case is a mix of both, something you need to do and something you enjoy doing. Instead of watching Netflix, which would have only given you temporary satisfaction, you are now also benefiting your physical health and mental health by socializing with friends while playing some ball. Living with purpose means you have your goals in mind with everything you do.

I recommend sitting down and asking yourself how you could put true purpose in your life. I realized that success is something I strive for, making this the outline of everything I do because it is always tied to my goal of success whenever I am doing something. Now, most people think I am referring to money when I speak of success, but my definition of success, as I've said throughout the book, is to make good money and be prosperous but live a healthy and happy life: Life of Balance.

Another concept you must understand is to lower your ego as well and have Self Understanding. Self-understanding is "the ability to understand one's actions and reactions" according to google. This means understanding what you are capable of doing and what you lack. If you lack the science aspect of things, are you going to pursue becoming a rocket scientist or pursue becoming a lawyer with a more robust background in reading, writing, and speaking? It would be best if you had self-understanding with everything you do. Everyone wants to say they are the best at everything they do when realistically, everybody has strengths and weaknesses. Man-up/ Woman-up and be able to distinguish your rights from wrongs, strengths from weaknesses so that you can have self-growth. Nobody is perfect, and everyone has their strong and weak suits.

I have a friend who claims he's the best at everything he does. I asked him," Hey, are you any good at volleyball? I have this tournament and am missing a player." He responds," David, people clap for me when I play volleyball; I'm that good." Obviously, I added him onto my team without thinking twice to eventually realize that my friend has never played the game in his life and is awful. He goes around with the mentality that he is the best but, in doing so, literally leaves him being the worse. Self-understanding yourself makes you better identify what you are good at and what you need to work on. Continuously saying you're the best at basketball, for instance, will tarnish your mentality and not leave you not as "hungry" to succeed and become better. So, while you say you're the best on your team, your teammates are working on getting better and taking your position.

I mean, think about it, how are you supposed to understand scenarios and other people when you are not even self-aware of yourself? Statistically, being self-aware means, you have higher emotional intelligence, linked to people making an average of almost $30,000 more, according to TalentSmart. This is because self-awareness leads to you taking advantage of your strengths and easing away from or improving weaknesses. Taking advantage of strengths and weaknesses, more money, more reliable and effectiveness, just overall more authenticity are all a few signs of benefits of being self-aware. So, the question now lies at hand, how do you become more self-aware?

I believe a big problem with people is that most people have such a high ego. People can't admit their wrongs and take their losses, making you look second-class. To grow, you must be able to understand and learn from mistakes, failures, and wrongs. Lower your ego and deal with your ego as it keeps you out of touch with the reality of things. For example, if I tell my friend that he needs to practice to sustain his spot on the basketball team, his ego gets in his way and prevents him from hearing the importance of my feedback. His ego makes him think he is the best and entitled to everything when this is not a sensible way of things. Being egotistical or full of oneself is not part of an accomplished mindset. You must understand that you have flaws, people are constantly competing with you, and there is always room to improve. Doing these things will make you a determined, hard worker and ultimately flourish.

Something else that holds people back is the lack of self-respect. Suppose your boss asked you to throw out the trash; you're throwing out the trash if your teacher tells you to move your moving seats. But if you said to yourself that you wanted to accomplish tasks A and B today, why didn't you? That's because of a lack of self-respect. There are many different ways to gain self-respect, being nice to yourself, constantly working on your goals but acknowledging that nobody is perfect, always tying in and prioritizing happiness in your life, establishing a purpose, workout, etc. Respect is given freely to nobody, not your parents, peers, or even yourself. However, respect is earned, so go out and earn your respect by working hard and accomplishing what you want to do.

Respect should be something you strive for in yourself but also from others. One way to earn respect from others is to respect other people. Doing this shows character and someone that people can rely on. Another way is showing consistency in everything you do, your promises, your actions, everything. A man's word is sometimes the only thing they have, so you lose respect when you say you're going to do something and don't do it. Striving to do better and admitting to your mistakes show that you're a humble, hard working person.

The definition of respect is admiring someone because of their accomplishments, abilities, and qualities. By definition, respect is given for doing things that others could not achieve (through arduous work) or just putting your time into activities to help others. To have that accomplished mind mentality, you shouldn't strive for respect but see it come as you continue throughout your days of accomplishing one thing after another. As Paulo Coelho once said, "Respect is for those who deserve, not for those who demand it." Do what Coelho said and go out there and earn your respect!

With respect comes confidence. If you're not doing things confidently, you aren't doing them to your full potential. Confidence makes us move forward with opportunities and allows us to cope better with setbacks. For example, I am making a non-profit now; my options are to pay thousands of dollars to a lawyer to help file all the forms or learn how to do it myself. I am constantly looking for the challenge of learning new things (mainly when it saves me thousands of dollars), but let me tell you; there have been a handful of setbacks with filing articles of incorporation, getting board members, handling social media, etc. Without confidence in myself to be able to move forward, I would have just failed and hired an attorney or given up on my dreams.

Now let's discuss failure, When the failure aspect of things comes in, failure is a lack of success, but to be successful, you must fail. If you aren't failing in the thing you want to succeed in, your goal isn't big enough because success never comes without failure. Failure is what causes us to strategize, think and reconsider what we should be doing to succeed. Failure teaches us to learn and grow and teaches people skills like being determined, putting effort, and even building self-esteem. In order to grow we must go through a catalyst of change, failures, success, which will in time lead us our destined path.

You must learn to embrace failure and grow from it, and to do this; you must have the confidence and determination to move forward. Some people crumble under the thought of failure while others flourish; the question now becomes, what are you going to do when things don't go your way? If you have that accomplished mind

mentality, the answer is simple, keep working and grinding until your

end goal is finally accomplished. Thomas Edison had 1000

unsuccessful attempts at inventing the light bulb. After every failure,

he was told that everything they did was in vain and they

accomplished nothing when Thomas had the accomplished mentality

and knew to keep going. A reporter asked Thomas Edison, "How did

it feel to fail 1,000 times?" He replied, "I didn't fail 1,000 times. The

light bulb was an invention with 1,000 steps." Think of failure as a

step in the process because experience, knowledge, growth, and

overall value come with failure. Experience because you now

understand what not to do/ an attempt that won't work, knowledge

because failure leads to accumulated wisdom that will lead to success,

growth because of how we mature, learn, develop from failure, and

with all these things bring value to oneself.

Now that the importance of failure is detailed, you must

understand ways to recover from failure. First, I would say "ignore

the haters" because people will always say, "I told you so," and if this

is a goal that you want to accomplish, keep pushing forward because everything comes with hard work and nothing is impossible. Next, would be not to crumble under failure but embracing it and realizing that it is a step in the right direction. Failure could also be used to push yourself to recover from it and propels you in the right direction, so make sure to use failure as leverage for yourself. Yet another way to recover from failure is revisiting your plan. Outlining your goals and objectives is probably one of the most important things to do when you are trying to succeed in something, but more times than not, you must revisit your outline and fix your plan when failure comes around. Sometimes, people's plans are not detailed enough or can not realistically get done the way they have imagined, so fixing it and altering it from your newly regained knowledge from failure will help you move forward. These are only a few ways to get better, but ultimately the only way things will get done is with your accomplished mentality; remember, failure is a vital part of the process.

Moving onto one of the most limited things in our lives, time. Everyone has spare time on their hands now the question is how do you spend it? Should it be spent watching Netflix, playing video games, or how about scrolling through social media? No, it should not. What you decide to do with your spare time can better you in ways you could never consider. There is a reason colleges value extracurricular activity in student college applications. Having positive extracurricular activities can improve time management, learning new skills/information, better social skills, boosted performance, etc. For example, if you are trying to better your health and enjoy the game of basketball, put 2 and 2 together and play some basketball. Doing so will improve your health from cardio and bring enjoyment to your life. Choosing to start projects or researching ways to build success is another good outlook. There are endless amounts of things you can do other than sitting down on your couch watching TV; find the ones you enjoy doing and will benefit you in some way; time is finite, and everything you do should tie into bettering ones-self.

The best extracurricular activities are ones that can teach you valuable skills. For example, if you have always wanted to learn how to work with computers, consider taking a class or watching free videos. Everything nowadays is becoming more accessible and easier to do. Back in the old days, if you wanted to be a writer, you would need to write a book, edit it, and submit it to a publishing agency, hoping they would publish it. Now, you can self-publish your work through amazon in kindle in a matter of minutes. The point is to go out and do whatever you desire but make sure it is valid and not wasteful.

A successful person tries to tie everything they do to an aspect that will help them throughout life. Extracurricular activities should be chosen wisely as anything else in life because they have a toll. More times than not, your extracurricular can affect your other aspects of life; if you choose to pursue writing in your spare time, it will help build your vocabulary and better your writing skills altogether. Now, does finishing Stranger Things on Netflix better you in any specific way? No. Choose what you do wisely because sometimes wasting your extra time on useless things keeps you away from being successful and slows down your productivity.

Now we discuss what I believe is the most important and best opportunity in life, education. School is imperative to be a successful person because most opportunities given in life run through education; 88% of millionaires graduated through college, which shows that education is nothing to be neglected but attended daily, early, and consistently throughout life. Our parents are our greatest teachers at the first level of education. Prenatal learning, like, taking care of the baby, avoiding stress, and taking care of the mother's physical, spiritual, and emotional states, are essential. Research has shown that learning starts in the womb, the mother's health is paramount, and it does not hurt to read, sing, and play music for the child in the womb. Learning starts further at birth, with stimulation of music, reading, playing, and generally interacting with mother and father is stimulating learning for the baby. As a toddle, prereading activity, music, and generally positive interaction with other toddlers and adults further the learning.

Elementary school is a fertile ground and, in fact, the foundation of learning. All pre-kindergarten, kindergarten, and elementary school teachers are the most essential learning segment. Elementary school is the foundation for all learning. This is when a good and dedicated teacher can make a life influence in the future of education. Whether one loves or hates learning or sees it as a task is based on those early influences. Falling in love with learning starts early in childhood and carries throughout life. Seldom will you meet someone whose love of learning and school did not create early on in his life. You don't develop a love of learning while in university, doing a full academic load and then doing lab work to meet biology or chemistry requirements. Therefore, the parents must be involved in the learning and school experience from the first start.

Parents need to demand excellence in education, devoted teachers, and schools that sustain and promote growth and learning. Mediocrity in education should never be accepted. If the teacher is not all in the child's education, they should look for work somewhere else. Having a teacher license should not be a union card, with full employment and a guarantee of employment for life. Schools need to excel, and parents should demand excellence in teaching and not tolerate any excuses. Failing schools need to be reassessed and make them fully productive or shut down.

Let's take a brief look at how many vital steps are taking place in elementary school. Love of learning is just one of many, and reading, writing, and mathematics play a crucial part. Being able to get along with others, following school rules, meeting deadlines are also important. The USA is clearly behind other developed countries, like France, in which children go to school for 240 days, and even on Saturday's morning. In Japan, school days are longer; children are demanded to clean and maintain their schools, serve their lunches, and attend school longer on a daily and yearly basis. The idea of having summer off to "work on the farm, planting, or working" must be terminated. We need to follow other developing countries' example and invest heavily in education, like longer school days, Saturday school, and 240 days a year of schooling. We spend less on education than most other developing countries on a per capita basis. Instead, we focus on being "the world's policeman" and spending more of our GAP in defense and providing defense for countries that can finance and defend themselves. Let's concentrate on our problems here and not be the "fireman who goes to put out fires when his barn is burning." It is time to shift from military needs to educational needs.

At the same time, middle school is also crucial. Middle school is a preparation for high school. A poor and deficient middle school experience sets the student for failure in high school. Let's take mathematics. Mathematics is based on a foundation. You can't step up the ladder if you fail the first rungs of that ladder or are not properly anchored. Success in high school in Algebra, Geometry, Calculus, and most sciences, like Chemistry, is based on a complete foundation in mathematics. High school teachers are right that they should not teach you percentile, fraction, or even long divisions when you start taking Algebra or Geometry. Class, the foundation of mathematics, the building blocks, must be obtained in Middle school. Administrators and parents must ensure that social and political influences do not overlook STEM courses. We must have daily teaching of STEM courses and not neglect them by social agendas and those that want to make schools the focus of indoctrination in social ideals dictated by a liberal. School is about academics' basics, not a social arena or a political place to indoctrinate students in perceived social agenda.

High School is "where the rubber meets the road." Yes, you should participate in social and athletic functions in high school but not lose track of learning and setting yourself up for college. Life will always throw distractions at you but staying true to one's morals and goals distinguish the rich from the poor and the successful from the unsuccessful. The football team or any other athletic team will not provide for your family or make you successful in college if you are missing foundations in academics. Many high school athletes find out when they get to college, or worse, when they finish college, they are prepared academically for college or work. Being offered a prestigious athletic scholarship will not help you if you have to drop out due to poor academics because you did not meet the necessary academic requirements in high school when you get to college. An SAT of 800 will not get you graduating from college, and an athletic scholarship will be worthless if you can't finish college and you fail due to poor academics. In the past, start athletes in college were "passed on" because of all the football team's prestige. Even now, some universities are misled into thinking that "a great football team, going to bowls, or even winning a state championship is a great and undisputed shining light for the university. Some universities pay their football programs an 8 million yearly salary, while the academic faculty are asked to "tighten their belt." Also, their football budgets exceed the entire yearly academic cost of running college as a whole; for example, a football budget of 20 million exceeds the educational requirement of the College of Arts and Sciences, usually ten times the fold. Make sure that academics are paramount in high school since your college success will be based on your foundation while in high school. Ascertain that you take four years of Math, including Algebra, Geometry, Trigonometry, and Pre-

Calculus. Also, take four years of English and Social studies. Two years of a foreign language. And, at least three years of sciences, including Biology, Chemistry, with a lab, and another two sciences. Don't neglect your academics in high school because of pursuing an athletic experience or social experience. Balance is key, but academics need to be paramount because they will serve you in life, with college, work, and general knowledge of life.

Now you're done with high school and have the power to decide what you want to do next with your life. Should you take a break before you move on to college? Absolutely not. Keep the momentum rolling and start building your resume by getting your AA, BA, and degrees after that. You must understand when getting a degree that it's best to get something with some power behind it. Many people say they want to be an entrepreneur, so they hop into attempting an MBA degree (Master of Business Administration) when this is a useless degree with no real job opportunities behind it. When you choose your degrees, you are choosing something that has a root to it. This means if you want to pursue business get an MBA in accounting which can also be used to get a job and bring stability rather than business administration which offers no real job opportunities after college. For instance, a degree in Business administration will help you understand how to manage a business better, but will people hire you? Most of the time, the answer is no; in fact, MBA degrees have a decline in jobs by about 34% (according to Forbes) which is even steeper than the national average of overall employment. Get degrees with some job opportunity behind them.

The reason most people work is so that they can make money. If you asked most people if they would continue working if they had all the money in the world, the majority answer would be no. So, choose a degree that is in an area you enjoy but will also bring in good pay. Saying you want to be a teacher is great until you are a teacher and realize how little they get paid. If you enjoy teaching more than law, but the choice is not something you would dread doing, the choice is simple. As mentioned earlier, life is a balance, and when making a choice determine how this will affect your balance. Doing something that you love but makes no money is not worth it. But being a test dummy for experimental drugs and getting made a load sum of money is bringing you anxiety, stress, and overall dreadful, is not worth it either. The choices you make in your early life will affect you for as long as you're alive, so make sure what you're doing will bring you a lifetime of happiness, success, and stability.

You have finished college or school and are in your first job. Congratulations, you are making money, living on your own, and planning the next phase of your life, adulthood. First, don't forget to get established in your work—volunteer to help the job and gain new skills or solidify your skills. Get to work 15 minutes ahead of everyone, be early always, and stay 15 minutes after everyone leaves. You will get noticed as dedicated to your job and your employer. Stay away from "sinking ships." Stay away from toxic people at work, like those who are unhappy, complaining, and not doing "their shares of work." is the advice my grandfather has always drilled in my head.

Pick coworkers carefully and realize that there is a difference between coworkers and friends. Friends are those with whom you share values and ideals, and you get together after work for play and dinner and are invited to their houses, and you feel comfortable inviting them to your house. Coworkers are people you work with and only have the job in common. They will go their own ways as soon as the job is over. Typically, coworkers are gone from your life after the employment ceases, for you or them. Also, bluntly put, don't get your meat, where you get your bread. As much as you can, don't have intimate relationships with coworkers, especially those you work closely with. Keep your personal life apart from work. This is important, and countless "work relationships" have ended badly. Be particularly vigilant about not having intimate relationships with subordinates, like those you supervise, mentor, or have supervisory capacity. This is common sense but particularly important in this age of "discrimination," whether real or imagined. Countless good people have been taken down from lifelong professions for reports of sex abuse. It is impossible to get from under these accusations, whether real, imagined, or predetermined for vengeance. You will have to leave with the permanent taint of being accused of sexual harassment at work, whether real, imagined, or done for personal vengeance. Circumstances now are that even the accusation of sexual harassment is career-ending, you are guilty, regardless of your innocence, and in fact, you are presumed guilty and not innocent. Most people have to quit their jobs or careers and move on, regardless of their involvement. Once accused, you are presumed guilty.

Life has many steps as you have read but if you go into something thinking you're not going to be able to do it effectively or succeed, you're not going to put your total amount of energy, therefore not being as effective. I mean, why would you? Putting effort into something you think you're going to fail is a waste. Recognizing that your mindset and how you think impacts you is crucial to success. One must have a positive outlook and be determined to conquer all obstacles in order to achieve greatness. The difference between the winners and the losers is that those on top did not in the first hurdle they phased. When listening to success stories of many CEO's or accomplished business people there seems to be one common denominator: perseverance. This thought carried some weight in my eyes because it made it clear that how you address things and your mentality differentiate millionaires from ordinary people. Realistically, most millionaires are self-made, so their fortune can't be considered inherited, so what made them rich? Their mentality and outlook of things did. To truly be successful, you must understand everything you do from your thoughts, tone of voice, representation, extra-circular, overall, everything, which will lead to your rise or fall.

To continue talking about how thought can affect someone, think about pride. Most people in the world want to be a leader, in control, or just the best, and it's this mentality that makes their dreams, dreams. Being too prideful is the demise of many people and often leads to poor choices. If you're a leader of a club and about to get voted out, you may start making destructive choices that can tear the club apart. Like, spreading rumors about other members so that they vote for you, in this scenario, this will tear the club apart from the inside out. This is one possible scenario out of millions, but it proves that being humble is more beneficial to living a life of success than being too prideful. One's way of thinking can play a significant role in their path to success.

Your thoughts can't be changed, but what you do can have a ripple effect. Something that holds people back is that they reminisce of the past when that does nothing but hold you back. If you and your friend got into an argument and parted ways, don't try to do things to screw them over or empower yourself over them; instead, keep accurate to yourself and morals. Your natural growth will show people that little can indeed affect you. Now when I say you shouldn't look back on the past, I'm not saying you shouldn't mourn good times or a loss of a loved one; in fact, not mourning a loss of a relative is inhuman to me; what I mean is you can't let it affect your overall way of life for extended periods. The past is just that; in the past, there is only one way to change a past grade or past event, go to your laboratory and invent a time machine, then go back and change what you want changed. Mother Teresa once said," Yesterday is gone; tomorrow has not yet come. We have only today; let us begin." This is nail on with my point that the only thing you can change is what's in front of you, so allowing the past to affect you is hurting your present opportunities and future ones to come. Grow from the past and do not let it hold you back.

It's sad to say, but being too nice will pave you to being used, mistreated, and overall unsuccessful in the world we live in. If you have a friendly and lenient boss, would you be stressed about not completing a deadline? No, you will abuse their actions/ kindness and continue to do things at your own pace rather when they should be done. A buddy of mine is too nice, and every time he is asked to do something, he complies as if he was a dog. He is constantly being asked favors like to be picked up or dropped off and does so with no hesitation because of his kindness being abused and his ability to say no. If you're going to live a life of success, you must understand that you're living for yourself and your family. There is no need to comply with other people's commands unless they put the food on the table. You must also be able to say, "No." There are plenty of scenarios to say no, and a common one is when asked to do a favor. I'm not saying reject every favor people ask of you but evaluate every favor you do for people by asking yourself what they have done for you, do they repay your favors, how often are you doing things for this person, etc. If you see that you constantly do something for them and aren't receiving much back in return, it's a matter of common sense that you should start using the special word," no."

People can heavily affect your way of life, and you can't let others have such a detrimental effect on you. When I say this, I'm referring to emotionally. I've lived through multiple betrayals, and every time it happened, I continued living the best I could. You have to acknowledge that no matter what happens (other than your death), the sun will rise in the morning and go down at night. The world will live on with or without you, so you must keep up with it and stay true to the path of success. I was discussing a scenario with a friend of mine in which she said that she stays home and doesn't socialize as much because her old friend group betrayed her. I tried explaining to her that she was wasting time and not living life to the maximum capacity in doing this. She was not only too nice (which they used to abuse her kindness), but she was too attached, which made it, affecting her ability to make new friends/ go forth and go deeper into relationships by socializing outside of school.

I repeat certain things multiple times so that while you read, they get instilled into your mind. LIVE FOR YOURSELF. Life comes around and goes around for everyone, but the only person who has control of your life is yourself. If you start giving others the power to control you, they'll do so to benefit them somehow while most of the time they are tearing you down.

This paragraph is one that is going to be practical and straightforward and not financially costly but seldom used and refused frequently. This is about asking for help. We forget that we "don't know it all," and someone else's voice, ears, and advice can be of invaluable help. Let's take the choice of college major. A student should decide early on a college major. It helps since many majors or college goals can have prerequisites, and sometimes we start in a major, less say psychology or education, and then realize that we are in business or accounting. Many psychology or education classes won't count towards engineering, business, or architecture degrees. A student can use two years of college exploring a major, and the courses taken will not count towards the requirement for, let's say, an accounting degree. This is costly and not cost-effective. If in doubt as to one's future career, it would have been prudent to solicit the help of someone to guide you. One can start by using self-guided career choices books, such as "the color of one's parachute," or many other self-guided books on choosing a career path. Most of the time, it is wiser to seek the guidance of someone trained to help students declare a major. A good career counselor will start by giving tests and assessing your interest and capacity to do certain majors.

Obviously, we tend to either be good at working with numbers and data, i.e., think of an engineer, computer programmer, or accountant, then working with people think of a teacher, a nurse, or a social worker and psychologist. Certain feelings require a solid basis in Mathematics and Sciences. For example, many students who want to be psychologists don't realize that psychology is a science and relies on statistics, think higher mathematics, experimental designs, again based on higher mathematics, and sciences like; brain anatomy and functioning, requiring knowledge of biochemistry, biological basis of behavior. The first two years in psychology are usually spent in the lab, running experiments, or in-class taking anatomy of the brain, biological basis of behavior, and just general biochemistry of the brain function. They think synapse, brain specialization of behavior, BROCA area dealing with expressive language, and other areas of the brain dealing with human behavior, short- and long-term memory, learning theories of brain-behavior, and Pavlovian basis behavior, brain injury changing personality and cognitive functioning. There are many students in psychology that decide to drop out or seek other academic areas with less scientific, mathematics, or sciences components and requirements. For some, the science of psychology based on biochemistry, biology, and statistics is a turn-off to the profession, which they thought dealt with "listening, advising, guiding, and providing succor" to needy people in desperate or traumatic situations. Every college has guidance or student guidance department, which can help you narrow your choices to your interest, desires, and capacity. For example, most people don't realize that being a psychologist requires four years of undergraduate, 4 to 6 years of graduate education, and a dissertation for the doctoral degree. Psychologists are not medical doctors but Doctor of Psychology, and the training in terms of longevity and difficulty equals any DO or MD professional degree. In addition, to be licensed in the USA, the person needs to have two years of supervised experience with 4000 hours of supervision, and then pass a state examination and a national psychology examination and exceed 50 to 75 percent of all questions in the exam depending on each state. Many roadblocks must be overcome, like matching a psychology residence, being successful at this residency, and passing the state and national exam. Some potential psychologists don't get a match to the desired area, location and, worse of all, fail the state or national exam and can't be licensed in the state they want to work.

A guidance professional at the university can do some tests, including the Self Help Test and the strong vocational test, which will help define your interest in a professional or career area. Further guidance will help you determine if you have the capacity and resources to finish a long, academically demanding study for 10(minimum) to 12(average) years of sole dedication to study. One also needs to look into the cost effectiveness of the career choices and current, and future work demands. Again, you don't want to study as a blacksmith when public transportation and personal cars are the forthcoming form of transportation, not horses. A trip to the guidance at your college early on as a freshman can pay invaluable returns in not wasting time, not taking courses that are not required or needed, and best of all, narrowing down your career choices to a realistic, doable job, with current demand and future job opportunity.

The guidance at most colleges also helps in times of crisis/self-doubts/ relationships/ emotional circumstances or just general adjustment to college. They can help with psychological support and guide you through different stages of your life in college, career, or relationships. When you start college, you will most likely be away from home—wee—but liberty also has responsibility. It would be best if you were independent. Tasks provided by parents like food on the table, transportation, set hours for study or sleeping, guidance with friends and other questions, and even laundry or what to eat, budgeting, planning, and dealing with school issues are your own now. Your parents will not be looking over your shoulders for typical daily activities, or the choices you make are going to be life choices, good decisions rewarded, bad decisions with consequences, and in general, the life you lead would be your own. Most first-year students have problems in this unique situation and life starting. The primary concern is not where to do the laundry, what to eat, or where to eat since many campus facilities are available; the problem is going to be relationships, the courses of study, and buckling up the hatches to deal with the course that you need to sail now and in the future. There will be stormy weather.

Broken and hurtful relationships, disappointments in people and situations, and just general life as it occurs. A helpful ear and a good counselor relationship can help deal with the stormy weather. Whether deciding a major, being in or terminating a relationship, and just general plans must be dealt with successfully and effectively. If at any time you need help, whether a sore throat, that could be strep throat, leading to severe problems if not treated appropriately, timely, and aggressively, ask for it. Minor physical and emotional problems can worsen if not treated. If you feel that you need help, ask for it. College also provides tutorials and help, with many having reading and writing clinics. Ask for help at the beginning of the course from your professor if you feel that you are not coping with academic demands. They are the first line of defense, and professors can help you by providing tutoring, advising of resources, or just generally advising that this course may not be suitable for you now, given other courses or issues in your life. A good rule in college is not to bite more than you can chew. The first semester you should only take four courses or 12 credits; starting slow in college is a good approach. You should not take more than five courses or 15 credits. Also, learn to balance your studies with easy and demanding courses; for example, if you need a lab for a course, make sure that the other three courses don't require a lab. Don't be afraid to drop a course if you feel that you are not prepared for it.

College is not a sprint but a marathon. The turtle, going slow but steady, will finish the race rather than the hare taking fast and quick sprints. If you are weak in Mathematics, don't take more than one math or science class at a time. There is no dishonor in finishing a Bachelors' degree in 5 or 6 years. If you can do it in 4 better, there is still no dishonor in completing 4.5, 5, or 6 years. Finally, strive for balance, balancing living activities like eating, exercising, work, academics, fun, partying, and relationships. Most people fail college due to poor financial planning, poor choice of majors, poor relationships, and failing to adjust to college life by having a preconceive unrealistic focus on one area, with partying, and not balancing the other regions. BEST of LUCK.

CHAPTER 4

MONEY CONCEPTS

This chapter unlike the last and is tuned in more on money/investment concepts. You can have all the characteristics of a rich successful man but without the ability to understand how to use and invest your money you will be left in an impoverished state.

Being smart with your money is a crucial necessity because to invest in yourself financially, you must first have the capital to do so. To be smart with your money, you first must understand what money does for you and its importance. Money realistically is paper with some ink on it. We put value towards this paper, and it does nothing more than give us a decision. You get to decide where you want to live, eat, how you want to dress, etc. Money is one of the most important factors of life as, without it, we would not be able to survive being hungry, homeless, and overall suffering. Money may be enjoyable and give you the ability to buy countless items. These things may be pleasant but preserving money and making "money-moves" is essential to living a life of balance. Making poor money choices will lead to instant regret, stress, and countless hours of working on getting more money.

Throughout the reading, you can tell that I value happiness and fun and believe that life is about enjoyment, memories, and satisfaction. Now, valuing these things does not mean going and eating $1000 meals when you have $10,000 in savings or taking out a loan to buy a $50,000 BMW to impress your friends. Instead, a rule of thumb says you should put 50% of your money to needs, 30% to wants, and 20% to financial goals (stocks, retirement, investment properties). Doing this makes it so that you are not constantly spending everything you receive.

For instance, let's use Mike Tyson; according to Forbes, he has made 400 million+ (which is about 700 million now because of inflation) and lost it because of his constant need to spend. Tyson had luxury properties, clothing, exotic cars, and things as ridiculous as a pet tiger. In 2003 he declared bankruptcy. Following the 50/30/10 rule, he would have been much better off than now (only worth about 3 million dollars).

Having nice cars and clothing may seem like a big deal at the time but only grants temporary satisfaction. Being able to save $50,000 and putting it into an S&P 500 ETF would lead to that $50,000 doubling in about 7-10 years (calculations based on the average return S & P had the last 100 years). While a car, the first five years devalues about 50-60% of the original purchase price. You also have to think of it in the hours you work. If you make 30 an hour, is it worth it to spend $50,000 on that car or, in hours, about 1667 hours of your life? This excludes all additional costs from owning the vehicle like gas, insurance, maintenance, etc.

I was driving around and saw a nice red Ferrari, and when I saw it, I said," oh, that is nice." Realistically, buying these flashy shoes and cars means nothing more to people than an "oh, that is nice." At the end of the day, it is better to be prosperous than look rich, so spend your money wisely rather than on stupid, flashy accessories. Being in a deep desire for validation in other people has been known to create many different health problems for people, including anxiety, depression, and much more. Validation is no more than acquiring someone's approval. Now the question lies, why would you want somebody else's approval? You are living life for yourself, so having someone tell you how to dress, act, and what to buy is useless. Now, don't get me confused; there is a difference between advice and validation. Take advice from people on topics you are unsure about, more critical and game-changing issues, or hear what people have to say and evaluate it afterward. Validation and approval of your ideas could be useful. However, validation is a tool that should be used at your discretion; make sure it is for the right reasons and wanting validation for everything you do is not righteous.

Being smart with money also includes investments. Only invest what you could afford to lose and diversify in your stocks to lessen the risk of losing it all (they say you should not have more than 5% in a specific stock). Also, choosing what to invest in, whether that is safe, moderate, or risky investments, there should be a percentage in each of these according to your age. For instance, someone who is 70 years old cannot afford to put their money into high-risk stocks as they do not have the time to coop if money is lost. Finally, investments should be researched heavily before clicking the "buy" button. Make sure to research what you buy and look for any form of news they have coming out like earnings reports, signs of drama, future releases of products, anything that could affect the stock for the good or bad. Hours should be spent researching before you make your final choice to invest, as you can make a fortune or lose a fortune.

Create a spending plan and budget, invest your money, save money, pay off debts; these are all ways to be smart financially. Losing money like Mike Tyson is one thing but spending money you do not have and being put in debt is another. Being in debt affects credit, which leads to not being able to get credit cards, loans, jobs, impairs the ability to make/ manage a business, etc. It is easy to spend money and hard to pay off money spent; debts add up and lead to one going bankrupt. Bankruptcy, in simple terms, is a way to be released from all the debts you owe, but the title of filing for bankruptcy can stay with you for about 7-10 years of your life. Getting into bankruptcy kills your ability to get credit cards, depletes your credit score, you will lose any property you own and the ability to take out loans. Simply take care of your credit because poor credit damages your image.

Having money gives you the ability to decide. However, challenging financial situations negatively affects health and often lead people to overwork to pay monthly bills. Stay out of being in a financial crisis and be smart with your money by watching what you spend your money on, saving, budgeting, investing, etc. Employers like financially responsible workers; if you remember anything from this book, remember that advice!

Now that we discussed being smart with your money to gain capital let's discuss the art of Early Investing. Ever talk to your grandfather and hear him say," I wish I started earlier." This is something I hear from every older person I have ever spoken with say. To think that you have much time ahead of you to make money and save is the wrong mentality because the earlier you start, the better off you will be. Let me give you an example; let's say that you made a safe investment into an S&P ETF 5 years ago; since then, it has gone up over 100%, meaning you would have doubled your money. The earlier you start, the more time you're allowing your money to grow. Compound·interest, in simple terms, is putting money into the stock market and keeping it in there for an extended period. In doing this, someone who invests $5,000 annually (with a 10% interest rate) for 49 years will have about $5,600,000.

Earlier in the book, the idea of time and investing was brought out. Somebody in his 70s cannot make their investments as risky since there is not enough time to recover if they lose. However, starting earlier makes you choose to make your investments riskier and maximize your chances of making money as you have more recovery time. Starting earlier also gives you more time to learn how to invest. Let's use the stock market as an example again; beginning to invest in your 40s and learning how to play around with the stock market can be risky and lead to loss. If you buy an option and don't sell it on time, you can lose all your money. So, starting earlier and learning the tips and tricks will help you make more and invest better throughout your life.

Early Investing has other benefits like becoming a creditor. So instead of taking out future loans since you have money invested, you can take it from there. Also, giving out loans to people and collecting interest can be a good Hussle. Another plus of early investing is starting your retirement plan. As earlier stated, $5,000 now will be $534,000 49 years later, around retirement time. Obviously, that is just your initial investment and will contribute more and make more throughout the years.

Money gives you choices as well, so investing your money early (in your 20s, for example) will provide you with the ability to be able to make more financial choices, like buying a house in your 40s. In addition, being smart with your money early on will teach you discipline with your spending habits and help you learn to cut back on non-essential things. All these things will put you a step ahead and better your finances. I bought and sold shoes, graphics cards, designer clothing, etc. I had something known as "cook groups," which gave information on how to resale items, and I charged a monthly renewal. I also bought, sold, and rented out sneaker bots and even did side work for my father. I made thousands of dollars and am choosing to save those thousands of dollars and put them into DOW, NASDAQ, and S&P ETFs and not touch them for years to come. I set a list of rules: I will only take the money out for business reasons like school, properties, stocks, etc. When the compound interest aspect comes in, my money should double every 7-10 years because the interest will be reinvested as previously mentioned.

Now, let's go back to our earlier examples, you are working and collecting a paycheck for your efforts of going to school, taking tests, internships, doing term papers, and getting on-the-job training. All your efforts are paying off in a solid paycheck. A good rule of thumb is to spend up to 50 percent of your check on necessities, including housing, medical care, entertainment, vacations, car expenses, and paying off your school loans. Your first purchases should be essentials and necessities you need to live. Housing is a necessity, plus the best investment since it appreciates in value and you are using it when living in it.

How do you pick your first property? The first thing is location, location, and location. You need to find a place close to work, access to public and other forms of transportation. The ideal location should not be more than 30 minutes from work. Obviously, factors play here. Is the commute by car, public transit, or walking or bicycling? In the "old days," people lived on top of where they worked or could walk or bicycle to work. The baker would have his housing on top of the baker, the doctor's home would have a consultation room, and the innkeeper would live at the inn. This was an ideal situation but changed with the car, and now people could live at a different location from where they work. With open and green spaces less congestion, the suburbs open a completely different place to live, and many people fled the cities. With the cost of commuting, workers have returned to the city to be closer to work or entertainment.

Now the internet has a profound way of how we work and where we work, just as much as the car did in the past. Choices are greater now, and workers who can work remotely could work in another city, state, or even another country and do all the work remotely. A friend of mine did college in Europe while enrolled at FIU, and my father does his job as a lawyer all through the home computer; this shows that the internet is changing the way work is getting done. This is great. Now, you don't need to be stuck in a congested or crime-filled city or even tolerate crazy weather, like cold, ice, or frequent rainstorms. Obviously, this is not a panacea since networking, building relationships at work, and other personal contacts are missed, resulting in a lack of mentoring, work cooperation, and in some cases, feeling or being out of the loop. However, this has created greater choices for living. The internet has made it, so a country house does not need to wait until retirement or living in a boat would be possible for some workers. Regardless, you will need to find a suitable location for your needs.

Schools, where their friends live, and afterschool recreational opportunities are also factors if children are involved. Let's say that you are a doctor; proximity to the hospital and your patients are important. The doctor does not want to be more than 20 minutes away from the hospital for early morning rounds, emergency, or staff meetings. Hospitals are not always in the best or most convenient areas. Some doctors have found it helpful to have a small apartment, either sharing with other doctors, close to the hospital, and a home, in a peaceful, secure environment where a family can thrive. Cost is also important, and a typical rule is not to exceed 4 to 5 times your yearly salary for housing; for example, if you are making 1 million a year, you can afford 4 million-to-5-million-dollar housing. This will need to be contrasted to other expenses, a few being office expenses, school loans, and family or child expenses. A recommendation is not to include school loans in this calculation since they are not a living expense but a business investment expense. School loans could be delayed or expanded throughout professional life. Moreso, Housing should be the first and most important decision, and this could make you money with housing appreciation or take you down with foreclosure and bankruptcy. Be careful, and don't bite more than you can chew. Best to buy a house that you can afford other than one you are constantly struggling to pay.

Another purchase should be transportation and a car. A car needs to be safe, reliable, and affordable. Insurance cost is based on those factors. A Porsche is a great dream car, but remember it does not reflect your worth, and in fact, it does not attract the necessary attention one needs. In fact, it does not make you a better or worse person. It shows your choices. Obviously, if you are successful and want to treat yourself without hampering your bank account and lifestyle, it is nice to have the ideal car you always dreamt about. Just remember the car does not appreciate in value, and when you drive out of the dealership lot, you lost 10 percent of the value, and don't believe the salesman pitch of "just a limited edition; most sought after; etc." An expensive and exotic car requires specialized tools to fix, specific mechanics, and costly parts to maintain. Typically, maintenance is much higher and more frequent than in an everyday vehicle. Exotic cars' engines are not engineered for long life and reliability and are geared solely for performance, requiring more significant maintenance costs and more frequent repairs. Also, complicated engines require a greater amount of time to repair. There is a saying that the exotic car owner is most happy when he gets the car but even happier when he gets rid of it. Do you want to be with that girl that only looks you up because of the car? Gold diggers are attracted to exotic cars like bees to honey. The first car should be reliable, safe, and inexpensive to maintain.

How do you find a good reliable car? Look for the car that sells the most, and you will find a Honda, a Toyota, or just an average American car. The car with the most units produced is likely to fit this need and niche. Now buying a car that is constantly breaking and does not have all the new safety features is not what I am saying to do either. All the newer cars have safety features that help you identify vehicles in your blind spots, let you know when you are close to hitting something, and some even brake for you if necessary (about to hit something). Investing in these types of cars not only helps you with your necessity of driving but helps you stay safe on dangerous roads.

Technology is yet another example of essentials used throughout your life. Buying a new phone every year may not be the best choice for people financially, but the truth behind it is that everyone uses their phones for hours a day, every day. To check stocks, research information, communicate, or just for entertainment. So, buying a new phone every few 2-3 years is a necessary expense.

Along with other technological purchases like a computer which is used for similar purposes but expanded usage as computers are used to make PowerPoints, word documents, just ideally more work oriented. You cannot stay with outdated technology that takes forever to load or just does this half as effective as the newer technology. Stay up to date with technology and consider it an essential investment as it is. Technology is viewed as essential parts of business and can be used as a tax write off so if you have a business, right off the technology and if you work for someone else then ask them for the technology pieces and 9 times out of 10 they will supply you with it.

To move forward, many purchases should be made for your health throughout your life. If you do not take care of your health, it will deplete rapidly, so make the necessary purchases to be healthy. Health includes many factors like getting fit. One way to get healthy is to work out, so investing in a gym membership or gym equipment for your home is a quality purchase. Spending more money to buy organic food is money well spent. A healthy diet can lead to substantial changes in your health as well. It's about 80% of what you eat and 20% what you do. This means that if you eat awful (even if you work out substantially) you will become unhealthy.

Health also includes sustaining or fixing your health when you are sick or injured. Some people try to work past their injuries or sickness, but this statistically makes it worse. Take the time to go to the doctor when necessary. I am a big gym rat (I go to the gym a lot), but when I started working out I used to do bad form with the bench press and hurt my wrist. I kept trying to work out even when my wrist was hurting and ended up having awful wrist pains to the point where I could not work out my upper body at all for three months. The point is: even though you think you could work past your health problems, you simply can't. When you see you are sick or injured, take the proper action right away to avoid the effects of longer recovery time or permanent injury.

Another purchase that should go without saying is making purchases to improve your education. The more knowledgeable you have about a topic, you will make better, more rational discussions that will lead to a better outcome. Higher education and credits also lead to more pay. Think about it from an employer's perspective: Do you want someone who is more educated or less? Since this person is more qualified, he deserves better pay as well. Education has been proven to lead to more pay, 88% of millionaires have gone to college for a reason.

Prioritizing things is another aspect of being accomplished. The truth behind it is that time in a day is limited, so you must prioritize some things over others. For example, let us say you have a paper worth 20% of your grade due the next day, but you also want to work out. Although working out is an important goal, the paper's importance outweighs anything else and should be looked at as the main priority. Also, why feed your limited time to a task that is not as important/ beneficial to you? Doing so is wasteful, so you must be able to distinguish what's more important to you and what would benefit you the most. All I could do is give examples and suggestions but, it takes you to take in what I am saying and use it. To distinguish what's important to you, sitting down and evaluating what needs to get done and how beneficial, urgent, and essential each task will help figure this out. For example, if I have a test the next day, want to work out, work on side hobbies/ businesses, and play basketball, it's clear that those things cannot fit into the manner of a few hours I have after school. What should I do about this, then? It's clear I must prioritize the things most important to me, which in this case would be studying and the gym.

Understanding that not everything needs to get done first is the key to success. Some people write down their daily list, don't complete it, then sleep feeling like a failure when they realistically did as much as possible. Just remember to work smarter, not more complex, and be balanced. Statistically, people try to do things that will be the easiest to finish because doing so will lead to immediate success and gratification when the importance of that task is not so significant. All your goals could be essential, and you could revolve your time around completing them but still end up not finishing because you chose to do the least important ones first and focused all your time on those. Long deadlines could also catch up on you and what ends up happening is that most people procrastinate and work on less important things using the excuse that it isn't due for a while. While this may be true, evaluate how important that task is and if it is essential, break that long deadline into shorter ones and, most importantly, just get started.

CHAPTER 5

TIPS TO SUCCESS

Life is full of surprises and there are plenty of different ways to be successful. Throughout this chapter tips and tricks will be taught and explained that will help you throughout your journey to a successful life.

Making a daily list of what you want to accomplish that day is a way to put purpose into your life because it will help you outline the plan to be productive throughout the day. Even in the process of creating this very book, I had it on my list of things to accomplish for the day, "write 1 page of the book at a minimum". But just because you have a list of things written, does that mean they will magically get done? The simple answer is no; you must have enough respect and motivation to get them done yourself. This is what living with purpose is all about. I had my list of things written to do for the day and reviewed it before heading to bed and realized there were numerous things left undone. So, I asked myself, "How was I supposed to take the time to accomplish this?". After asking myself this question, I realized that I was constantly on my phone watching Tiktok for about 2 hours throughout the day, but the peculiar thing was I could not recall what I was watching. There was no true pattern or purpose for those endless hours I was spending on social media. I analyzed my behavior and modified what was keeping me away from accomplishing my daily goals, bringing temporary enjoyment and no purpose to help fulfill my life's goals. I understand that these things ease the mind and lead to healthier mental health but, there are plenty of other activities/ things to do that will ease your mind and bring productivity towards helping you grow, and the key is to find out what they are. To move away from these unproductive traps, I do a few things: gym, sports, reading, writing, researching (business things generally), or work. There are countless productive things to do you must find what fits you.

Everybody talks the talk; the question is, are you going to do it? Anybody can write out some goals on a paper and outline precisely what they will do but still not do anything. As long as success is something you strive for, your biggest friend but the worst enemy will be hard work, determination, and action. You must have the will or determination to take the first step to get something done because they say the first step is always the hardest to take. However, once that step is taken, everything after that is manageable. Let me give you a few business examples; getting to your first million is always the hardest because you did not have as much help, support, or resources as you have on your way to your second, third, and fourth million, etc. Purchasing your first property is also the most nerve-racking because of the paperwork, loans, wanting to pick the best destination, but once it is done, going onto the next one is a more manageable load. In scientific terms, there is zero momentum when you start, but as you continue to move forward, the momentum picks up, and the process goes by faster and faster.

Once you have the determination to take action, all that is required is hard work and consistency. If success came easy, then everybody would be successful; but success requires time and sacrifice.

Oftentimes top leaders have a common trait and that is the constant need to be better and compete with people surrounding them for the top spot. Does doing this sound easy? No, it requires hard work to have any success in your life. People do not understand that working hard for a week or two at a new job may impress your new boss right off the back, but inconsistent results will lead to immobile success. Anybody can go to the gym and do the best workout known to humanity, but the results will never be shown if they are not consistent. Back to the scientific way of things, the consistency develops the routines we need to be successful and builds momentum. Consistency leads to better results, efficiency, improvement, and overall success. An accomplished mind does not just decide to work hard one day and not the next; an accomplished mentality leads to constant hard work every day they can.

Another tip is this, do not be easily brought to your knees due to religious frauds. Religion is one of the most crucial things in one's life but wars have been fought, and countless lives have been taken for beliefs in different things. People take the power of religion and try to control you, so the first rule is avoiding false prophets. Faith in America is not regulated, and the idea of "separation of church and state" is a good idea and one we all should support. Unfortunately, charlatans and false prophets have used this constitutional ideal for self-aggrandizement, becoming rich, and generally abusing a vulnerable population, always at a most severe vulnerability in their life. People lean towards the church or religion in general when times are hard. Make sure you're not putting time and money into false prophets. One can only think about the Indian Guru in Oregon, with his propensity for the flesh, and he did not only have one Rolls Royce but over 50 Roll Royce's, acquired by lies and misperception of his "need." We can also think about the TV preacher, who indicated that "If Jesus came back, he would not ride in a donkey," and this was his assertion to request a 3rd private jet at the cost of millions of dollars. All these are just simple facts of "abusing" the "separation of church and state" to enrich, avoid taxes, live a flagrantly permissive and financially selfish lifestyle at the cost of the most vulnerable believers in our society. Violations have occurred economically and in exploitative relationships. There have been many cases of abuse of women, young men, and overall complete disregard for laws, the severe pedophiliac tendency with children, and misogynistic ideas with women. The state's hands are tied until the abuses violate the most vulnerable women and children. In some tragedy and unfortunate cases, this has resulted in "mass poisoning and suicides" and battles with the government trying to protect the innocent. The doctrine of separation of church and state has given these despicable sociopaths a way of violating women and children and enriching themselves without government oversight. Be careful of "new religions and the false prophets," who are more interested in pocketing your money for self-aggrandizement and enrichment than serving God's will. To many, we are "God's children," and his message is simple: obey the ten commandments given to Moses, love your fellow man, and treat people the way you want to be treated.

Impressive edifice, holding a church, a preacher flying in 3 private jets, and living a rich life at the cost of others does not impress me. Be careful of false prophets, especially those who try to divert you from your goal or separate you from your family and tell you that the church and the congregation is your true family and tells you to shift from being a doctor, a teacher, or just your work and if you have any wealth to give it to the church. These are red flags of false prophets and sociopaths trying to enrich themselves at your cost. Be especially careful of those who tell you that "religion is the opium of the people." True religion is to advance man and protect the vulnerable and the environment. Those who wish for a world without faith or religion have caused misery, poverty, executions, and mass imprisonment of the faithful. Look at Russia, where millions died out of starvation and executions and civil wars due to "religion is the opium of the people ."Look at the Jihadists, who have tried to kill Christian and Jews for hundreds of years due to the belief that "if you don't convert to their version of Islam, you are a heretic, whose only choice, by them, is decapitation Also, let's not forget the protestant and catholic wars in which mass killing and executions brought Europe from enlightenment to the dark ages. Religion has its fanatics, and we need to be careful not to give in to its dominions.

Let us use Catholics as an example; all you must do is have God in your heart, follow the ten commandments, and do unto others as you would have them unto you. Be careful of religion in college, particularly if they try to induct you by brainwashing and take you away from family, friends, and goals of being independent and successful. College campuses are "recruiting grounds for false prophets and their minions." This is because college is filled with uncertain people and others try to take advantage of people when they are weak or insecure, do not let them get you. Remember to study and reach academic and professional goals in college and high school. Don't be distracted by false prophets and look for the red flags mentioned like, "this church is your family; you must devote yourself to the church and forget about goals; your only goal should be the church. "Countless lives have been lost to false prophets and cults. People use the church, or just religion in general, to bring you into their operation and drain you of your resources/time. Anybody will use any excuse to try to prosper themselves, even using your believed god as a way to drag you in. Remember, there is only one person you can truly trust, yourself.

To move on, too much of anything is a bad thing, too much water leads to kidney problems, too much work leads to stress (which has its own set of health problems), even too many carrots can lead to skin discoloration. The point is, striving for success is one thing, but keeping true to yourself and your morals must be done to get to your level of accomplishment. Some people cut off everybody, revolve around work, and have no fun or experiences to attempt success. That is nothing more than a waste of time and a harmful example of success. Success is never-ending and can happen in many ways, but people strive to gain more and more to the point that it is harmful. For instance, some people want easy money, so they start committing illegal activities such as fraud or theft to gain some money. Doing these illegal things is morally wrong and can eventually lead to consequences. Success never comes easy, nor anything good in life, so work hard, be consistent, and receive results.

Moving onto your next tip, earnings. Your earnings at work have to be used appropriately. First comes housing, which should be your primary goal with work earnings. You should make housing the first priority and look into buying a house, condo, or a living once you settle at work for at least a year and have a down payment for housing. The house cost should be between 2.5 to 3 times gross earnings minus debt that you have, excluding student loans—these are considered business loans and should be treated as such. The place where your lives need to be safe, close to work, and in a growing community with parks, good schools, and neighborhood safety. A walk around the neighborhood should make you feel at ease, completely, and not having to look over your shoulder. Your neighbors should share your values or, at least, need to feel comfortable around them. Your home will be the most important purchase in your life. It is also the safest and best investment. You will typically see your home increase in value at the same time while you are using it. Also, plan carefully where you buy, and check for location, location, location. You want the best location that you can afford, a good location in the neighborhood, or a good condo with a good view and a location in the building. Also, it would be best if you bought what you can afford but with a view towards the future. For example, if you want to get married and have children in the future, you need to plan accordingly. Will the home fill your needs now, but how about the future? The Bachelor's pad in a swinging part of town, with bars, nightclubs, and restaurants nearby, is not the best option when you have a kid starting school, and you need a solid school system and a nearby safe school with an outstanding reputation. You don't want to pay a high mortgage and then pay high tuition for private school because the school system is a mess where you bought. Also, you need space to grow within your budget. A studio will not do it when you plan to get married and have children. At a minimum, you should look for a place to fill your needs down and at least ten years down the road. This means sacrificing "party and travel money" for housing and at least a two-bedroom and two-bathroom condo or house in most cases.

The second necessary purchase is transportation. You need to be close to work, family, and recreational areas, restaurants, places of the workshop, and just general park and recreation. You should not be more than 30 minutes from work. The first choice in a city with good transit should be within walking distance of the train or bus station. Even better, as people are returning to the town to be able to bicycle, scooter, or walk to work or a combination with mass transit. Regardless, you are likely to need a car. Make sure you buy something practical that fits your needs now and for at least six years, the typical life of a car. Cars are made for transportation and getting from point A to B. The Ferrari and Porsche may get you there but at a high cost. Cars are status symbols in our society, but be careful of conspicuous consumption, "buying to show off rather than a necessity." Driving a Bugatti is not going to make you a better person. Sports cars have higher maintenance and higher depreciation, tend to be less safe, and are a magnet for "speeding tickets" and getting into trouble. The public, particularly cops, has developed an idea of people driving those cars, such as "drug dealers, unscrupulous or loose and wild ." Having a fancy is not going to make you a better person. You want to develop yourself and be attractive to others by hard work, honesty, kindness, and be absent of jealousy and greed. A car may get someone's attention but won't hold it. Moral values will last and hold genuine emotions of decent people. You don't want to be surrounded by syncopating or those "getting juice from you." Once the juice is dried, they will quickly move to another source or look for a "sweeter or more abundant juice." These "juicers" are people you don't want in your life. All relationships are partially based on self-interest; make sure that your interests are also met. It does not have to be 50/50, but you need to get as much from relationships as you put in.

Be wary of conspicuous consumption in your life, whether it is a car, clothing, or relationships around you. There is something to be said about a simple, honest, and mature lifestyle. The fancy cloth, the sneakers, or the name brands will not make you a better person. Only hard work building your values, life, and morals do so. Vanity is a potent elixir that gets people drunk momentarily and causes troubles. Look at people like Epstein and Maxwell with their rotten, privileged lifestyle at the cost of innocent lives. And yes, full of private jets, private islands, and exclusive residences but devoid of values. Clearly leading to moral oblivion and decadence, and justly in their cases, jail. Money is valuable and needed and helps support your family. But it can't be an end in itself. Values are more important. In my lifetime, I have seen the unscrupulous pay dearly for the extravagant lifestyle and its excess. Jails are full of people paying dearly for their crimes of pulling "unscrupulous scams." Don't be caught in easy money or scams. Values and building yourself to be respected, hardworking, honest and kind, and devoid of jealousy and greed is imperative in life. The function of man is to live, not to exist. One shall not waste days trying to enrich oneself at the cost of the soul, and to prolong life by greed, is not a use of time.

The word investment is the word of the book. As you can tell throughout the book, the word "investment" is used a plethora of times. The reason for this is that every aspect of your life should be viewed as an investment and be protected. Your health is a significant investment, happiness, assets, stability, even your relationships. Everything should be looked at with the question, "How is this helping me?" If something is taking up time and not bringing back any return, why continue to do it? Many people think that investments are money-based because they only value money when there are many things worth more than money, one being time.

Everyone has a different perspective of what is right and wrong in life. Our perspectives shape how we make decisions and react to different experiences in our lifetime. Teens and young adults need to understand that finding balance in their lives and having a successful career requires them to say no to situations that will have a negative impact on their lives. Remember, you have choices in life, and you are the one making those choices. To achieve your goals and be successful, you need to be committed, motivated, work hard, set your goals, and learn from your mistakes. Keep a positive attitude and stay focused. Try not to be distracted from your goals by getting involved with drugs, alcohol abuse, or scams involving illegal activities. That can ruin your chances of having a successful career and life.

Many teens and young adults think that you need to make money quickly and easily to be successful in life, but that is not the case. They are looking for ways to make an easy buck and end up getting involved with scammers, drug dealers, or getting engaged in fraudulent activities that land them in jail. They are easily convinced by con-artists, so call friends through peer pressure, co-workers, drug dealers, in doing illegal acts that are not presented as crimes or losing money to scammers. Teens and young adults need to understand that scammers are trying to steal your identity to use it to commit illegal activities. Your life can become very complicated if your identity is stolen and can affect your chances of getting business loans, home loans, credit cards, and it can take a long time to clear your credit records.

Here are some examples of life situations that can get teens or young adults into plenty of trouble and complicate their lives. Dealing with so-called friends asking you to do them a favor can become problematic. Your so-called friend tells you to take a package to an individual you don't know, and he will pay you $200 bucks. You take the package to the address he gave you, and all of a sudden, you are surrounded by the police and charged with trafficking drugs and end up serving jail time.

A so-called friend asks you to take a suitcase for him while you are vacationing in Columbia to his mother in Miami, and he will pay you $500. You get to the airport and go through the screening process, and then the TSA enforcement person pulls you aside and tells you to follow him to a tiny room where they interrogate you and tell you they found cocaine packages inside the sole of several lady shoes inside the suitcase your friend gave you. They charge you with the procession of drugs.

A so-call friend tells you to pick him up at the airport. You drive to the airport and pick him up. Immediately you are surrounded by DEA agents. They arrest you and your friend. Both of you are charged with drug trafficking. Your friend was a known drug trafficker the DEA agents had been following for a while. Your so-called friend testifies against you later in court to get a reduced sentence and states that you were part of the trafficking deal. He cuts a deal so he could serve less time in jail. He gets six years in jail, and you get 15 years. In this life, you will discover you can't trust everyone and need to be careful whom you choose as your friends. Having a criminal record can have consequences later in life and can, unfortunately, continue to impact your life even after serving your jail time. For example, having a criminal record can make it more challenging to apply for employment and affect your family life later in time.

In this scenario, you are dealing with a con-man. You posted on the internet you are selling your car and are asking for $15,000. Someone responds and says they are interested in buying your vehicle and making arrangements with you to buy it. He says he will mail you the check to hold the car for him and pick it up in a week. He sends you the check, but the statement is for $19,000. You call him back and tell him he made a mistake, and the check is $4,000 over. He tells you to send him a check for the $4,000. He cashes the $4,0000 check, and by the time the check he sent you for $19,000 goes through the bank, it bounces. You end up losing the $4,000 you sent him. In other words, be careful whom you deal with on the internet, don't think everything through the internet is legit.

To be successful in life, you need to stay away from substance abuse (drugs and alcohol). Teens and young adults who get involved with drugs or alcohol abuse could ultimately commit illegal activities, landing them in jail or dying. Substance abuse can have a significant impact on your health and well-being. It can affect the growth and development of teens, especially brain development, and it can cause health problems in the future, such as high blood pressure and heart problems. The younger the teens start using drugs, the greater their chances of continuing to use the drugs and developing long-lasting issues in life. Actions have consequences.

Getting teens and young adults involved with drugs is a way drug dealer use to take advantage of teens and young adults by getting them addicted to drugs. This can land you in lots of trouble and even serve time in jail. Becoming a drug addict or alcoholic could end you with a lifetime of misery. Trying to balance your life also includes knowing when to say no. Peer pressure can be a challenging situation for teens and young people. Teens and young people want to be accepted and to fit in. For example, a group of friends is at a party, doing drugs and trying to incite you through peer pressure to use the drug. You need to have a strong will to say no, I am not using drugs. Someone in that group could be trying to get you hooked on drugs. These are drug dealers trying to make a buck, and the more people they get hooked on drugs, the more money they make. Once you are hooked on drugs, you could end up stealing from your family friends, breaking into cars, robbing to buy the drugs, and eventually serving time in jail. In other word's be aware of these techniques used by drug dealers and learn to say No. Don't let peer pressure make you do something you will regret for the rest of your life. Remember this keep vultures and thieves at your back, fly on the wings of angles.

Alcohol abuse is another way teens and young adults can get themselves in trouble, cause health problems, and end up doing illegal activities to buy alcohol. When teens and young adults start drinking at an early age, their chances increase of getting addicted to the alcohol and continuing to abuse it throughout their life. Alcohol abuse can lead you to develop chronic diseases such as liver disease, strokes, and cancer and can affect your mental health well-being over time, causing mood changes, anxiety, insomnia, sexual function problems, and problems with memory. It can affect part of the brain that involves sensory perception and muscle control. The Centers for Disease Control and Prevention (CDC) has defined moderate drinking as one or fewer drinks each day for women and two or fewer drinks each day for men. Alcohol abuse in teens and young adults can cause changes in mood that can affect their coordination and can affect their judgment and behavior that can cause them to commit illegal acts or cause car accidents, with injuries and death to innocent people.

Let me give you an example of how your life can change instantly because you made the wrong decision and are involved in a car accident while driving intoxicated with alcohol (DUI). You go to a party and drink all night excessively long. You decide to drive your car home even though you are intoxicated. You drive the wrong way in the expressway and hit a car, killing two young kids. You are picked up by the police and charged with DUI involuntary manslaughter. Your whole life is about to change for one wrong decision that you could have prevented. You are now looking at spending probably over ten years in jail plus penalties and up to fifteen years of probation; knowing when to stop drinking while in different situations is important. The best thing to do is not to drink and drive or have a designated driver take you home. You can also call a taxi or uber. There is no excuse to drink excessively to the point that you are drunk. Think wisely before you take those extra drinks. Remember, you have choices.

In life, there are many unscrupulous fraudsters (Swindlers, Scammers) waiting for the right moment to scam people. Teens and young adults need to understand these fraudsters are out there ready to convince you to get involved in some activity that is too good to be accurate and can land you in jail or are out there waiting to steal your identity and use this information to commit fraudulent transactions in your name. Millions of people in the U.S. are affected by identity theft today, which could have been prevented by being careful with your personal information.

Fraudsters can steal your identity by using your name, Date of birth, and social security number or getting your financial account numbers. By using this information, criminals can create credit cards, steal your money, take out loans and use your name for illegal purchases and fraudulent transactions, etc. So never share your personal and banking information, not even with friends.

Criminals use several techniques that you need to understand to prevent an identity thief from happening to you. Some of the methods used by thieves to steal your personal information are as follows, skimmers devices, mail fraud, internet fraud, Employment scams, Prize, sweepstakes, and lottery scams, stealing your purse or wallet, social media scamming, online retail scams.

Skimmer devices allow thieves to steal your credit card information and use it for fraudulent activities. When you slide it into a card reader at gas stations, ATMs, and other places, the device reads the magnetic stripe on your credit card or your debit card. It can happen when you use your credit card at restaurants, grocery stores, shopping stores, hotels, gas stations, just about any place.

Once they have your credit card information, they use your information to charge fraudulent charges online or over the phone; they can sell your information, create counterfeit credit cards, and load it up with thousands of dollars. Call the credit card company immediately and report it if this happens to you. They will cancel your credit card and issue you a new card. It's essential to review your credit card statements constantly. There are some contactless credit cards. For example, Apple Pay is a contactless system. No one touches your credit card, and you can pay with just a touch.

Scammers also use social media to trick teens and young people to provide personal information, which they use to commit identity theft. Social media have become popular hangouts for scammers. Many scams take place through online retail ads. You need to be careful when ads offer you free items and require you to fill out forms asking you for your name, Date of birth, address, and social security number. Check out the company name before you buy based on an ad on the internet.

Remember, many scammers are waiting for the right moment to convince young adults to sign documents that can later get them in trouble. Scammers want you to sign illegal documents quickly before you even have a chance to read what you are signing. Then, they convince you to provide your personal information, which they use in illegal transactions. In other words, be careful what you sign and be alert that scammers exist and are waiting for the right person to scam. Don't sign if you are unsure or feel uncomfortable signing any documents. Protect yourself.

Take, for example, a person you thought was a good friend who asked you to give him your personal information for him to apply for a mortgage loan in your name. He tells you not to worry that he will pay for all the expenses in obtaining the loan and pay for all the mortgage, taxes, and insurance. He will pay you $5,000 for helping him apply for the loan in your name. He tells you it's all legal. The bank approves the mortgage loan. Later he defaults on the loan and disappears. Meanwhile, you are responsible for the mortgage payments, and the property value has gone down in price. The bank refers you to the FBI. Guess whom the FBI comes looking for, yes you. Your job position and income were falsified in the loan application you signed. Your income and assets were inflated to qualify for the loan. All the documents turned over to the bank were falsified. You signed all the documents. The information provided in the financial part on the loan application you applied for was all false. The FBI comes knocking on your door and begins the interview process. The FBI informs you that they are investigating you for mortgage fraud. Mortgage Fraud is the intentional misstatement, misrepresentation, or omission of information provided to lenders or underwriters to obtain funds to purchase or insure a loan. Falsifying information on a mortgage loan application could land you serving years in jail. If the information provided on the loan application had not been falsified, you would never have qualified for the mortgage loan, and the bank would never have approved the loan. Mortgage fraud is a grave crime. Now the property you purchased is defaulted and foreclosed by the bank. Your credit is ruined, and you are convicted of mortgage fraud. Be careful what you sign, and don't let anyone convince you it's legal to give your personal information for them to apply for any loans.

In conclusion, life is complicated, and you need to be aware of the consequences of dealing with difficult situations to live a successful and healthy life. Life throws you curveballs, and you need to learn to deal with them positively to live a productive life. Life brings many obstacles and brings an abundance of risks. You will get a greater appreciation of life-based on making the right decisions and holding yourself accountable for achieving your goals. It's essential to understand your goals to be successful, but you don't want to overwork yourself or burn yourself out trying to achieve them. While on this life journey, enjoy yourself, keep yourself healthy, and have fun. You only have one life to live!

CHAPTER 6

FINALE

At the end of the day your life is in your hands. Some people have all the tools to succeed but don't want it enough. Life in no shape or form is easy and as soon as that becomes evident and you start working towards your goals, is the second you will start accomplishing things. Throughout the book you read an array of concepts, tips and information that will be useful throughout your life only if you enforce it. These tips are supposed to open your eyes to a new paradigm and help you grow as a person.

If you learn anything from this book learn that Living with the mentality of always bettering yourself and living with balance is the way life must be lived. To do so, understand what success is, live healthy, happy, and accomplished and follow the significant tips said throughout the pages. Remembering these tips while they happen throughout your life is crucial to stay away from sinking. Being successful is a lot less what you do but how you do it so make sure to comprehend these concepts so that you know how to deal with the roadblock when it eventually presents itself

ABOUT THE AUTHOR

David Duran Echavarria

Scholar, Entrepreneur, Philanthropist, and now Author is, to say the least, about David Echavarria. David Echavarria was born and raised in Miami, Florida and has always had an accomplished mentality. David was running businesses, making money, learning how to market, manage a business, project-manage, even file taxes, and create legalized businesses at an early age. In addition, David was part of an International Finance Academy for three years. This, along with his business experience from many past/ on-going projects, gave him the entrepreneurship knowledge and urge to write and inform people by creating, The Dawn of Success.